Conflict Management Coaching

The CINERGY™ Model

CINNIE NOBLE

2012
CINERGY™ Coaching

CINERGY™ Coaching
Phone: 416-686-4247
Toll free (Canada & US): 1-866-335-6466
Fax: 416-686-9178
Email: info@cinergycoaching.com
Web: http://www.cinergycoaching.com

Copy editing: Francine Geraci
Production editing: Jim Lyons, WordsWorth Communications
Proofreading and indexing: Paula Pike, WordsWorth Communications
Text and cover design: Tara Wells, WordsWorth Communications
Cover: Art by John Felice Ceprano http://www.jfceprano.com/

ISBN 978-0-9877394-0-7

To the many memories of
my beloved parents
Victor and Pearle Noble
and
my dear friend Max

Contents

CHAPTER 2
Conflict Management: There Is No Rule Book, 39

CHAPTER 3
Client Engagement, 83

CHAPTER 4
The CINERGY™ Conflict Coaching Model, 109

CHAPTER 5
Conflict Management Coaching Skills, 149

CHAPTER 6
Applications of Conflict Management Coaching, 189

CHAPTER 7
Measuring Conflict Management Coaching, 207

APPENDIXES

INDEX, 255

List of Figures

Foreword

Over the years, on my own journey of celebrating the growth of the field of coaching, I have been in constant awe of coaches who apply their expertise in different ways. One way is by creating new applications of coaching. These applications ultimately result in different "specialties" for helping clients optimize their potential in various aspects of their personal and professional lives. Upon creating these innovative programs, many coaches generously share their concepts and ideas with others. This is what Cinnie Noble has set out to do and has successfully accomplished in her book on conflict management coaching.

Coaching itself marries many different theories and areas of practice. Cinnie's work has solidly brought together two of these influencing areas that are clearly made for each other. Bringing the "coach approach" to mediation, and mediation skills to coaching, is a brilliant move. The integration of these two approaches, supported by a number of neuroscience principles, offers an effective and sustainable way to help people find their way through conflict.

For coaches who commonly assist clients with their interpersonal conflicts, it is especially helpful to learn more about how to do so by being able to use a process such as the seven-stage CINERGY™ model. All of us individually encounter conflict in our own lives, too. It is this fact that enlists much of my support of Cinnie's work. She believes that an integral part of a coach's personal and professional foundation includes conflict competence. This requirement makes perfect sense to be able to coach clients effectively in their efforts to gain the knowledge, skills and abilities to engage in conflict. And indeed, modeling solid skills of this nature in our own relationships contributes to the success of all our work as coaches. Thus, having a clear conflict management skill set is an asset on many levels.

Having an evidence-based structure, founded on rigorous study for conflict management coaching, is a gift. Coaches, mediators and others will reap the benefits of Cinnie's commitment to this specialty. Cinnie's clearly outlined concepts and examples are accessible and relevant, as are the range of specific skills, pertinent ROI suggestions, ethical considerations and client engagement ideas. And she shares her extensive knowledge and experience from her heart.

It is clear, on my reading of *Conflict Management Coaching: The CINERGY™ Model*, that Cinnie cares that we pay forward our learning, to make conflict an opportunity for growth and development for our clients.

> Pamela Richarde
> Master Certified Coach
> Former President, International
> Coach Federation

Foreword

We are delighted to introduce this important new book by our friend and colleague, Cinnie Noble. Cinnie's work as a conflict practitioner—a mediator, trainer and advocate—is already well known. Her new book is a vital contribution to the development of a field in which she is a pioneer—conflict management coaching.

The growth of one-on-one conflict management coaching as a discrete service offered by conflict practitioners reflects the changing landscape of dispute resolution. Much of this change relates to the role of the justice system in resolving conflict. A long-standing faith in the legal system and in lawyers as the champions of rights has been gradually replaced by skepticism about the costs and efficacy of legal solutions and adjudicated outcomes. Lawyers are no longer the "go-to" professionals for problem-solving—instead, they are often seen as an expensive way of escalating a conflict.

There has been a spectacular rise in the volume of self-represented litigants, many of whom do not see lawyers as adding value to their outcomes. Corporations have started to opt out of traditional dispute resolution systems, instead using private arbitrations and commercial mediation, hiring in-house counsel to settle disputes, appointing ombudspersons and instituting internal conflict management systems.

Conflicts deplete energy and resources and distract focus; at worst, they permanently destroy relationships. Litigation almost always produces these results. Increasingly, corporations and individuals are asking how to deal with conflicts so that problems are addressed and relationships are preserved. This shift has led to a quest for better ways to anticipate problems, take preventive action, encourage a cooperative approach to problem-solving and empower those in conflict to participate directly in resolution efforts.

Failing faith in traditional legal models of dispute resolution has occurred at the same time as the rise of the Internet, which has profoundly altered and reshaped the public culture of disputing. An entirely new medium of communication is emerging—email, texting, social networks, Skype and other Web-based processes—that challenges how we think about and process conflict. Access to information is changing the way we value (and how much we are willing to pay for) technical advice, whether offered by lawyers, doctors, financial specialists or others. We often feel that we have many (free) resources for information; what we need instead (and might be willing to pay for) is help with strategy, decision-making and planning. This shift is changing the nature of professional advice-giving and marketable services, and not only in conflict resolution.

Into this changing landscape comes the phenomenon of conflict management coaching. What has not changed is the continual presence of conflict in our lives—in our workplaces and families, in our communities and in the international world order. The conflict resolution field has developed a range of powerful intervention tools over the past 30 years, including mediation, collaborative law practice, facilitation, restorative justice and case management. These approaches have helped many disputants handle their conflicts more effectively, rapidly and humanely. But each of them depends on the intervention of a conflict professional into the conflict interaction itself.

There is an important gap here that Cinnie's book addresses in an elegant and practical way. We need approaches that will help people increase their capacity to handle their own conflicts, not only specific disputes but in the general capacity of individuals and organizations to anticipate and manage the full range of conflicts that they are likely to face. This information is relevant to managers, workers, union leaders, teachers, parents, divorcé(e)s, government officials, families and individuals—indeed, all of us.

Conflict management coaching offers individuals the opportunity to anticipate, strategize and operationalize how they will respond to conflict, whether in a personal or a professional context. It assumes that individuals can learn how to manage conflict better in their lives and to do so through dialogue, wherever possible, rather than working through proxies, employing third parties or using legal procedures. It further assumes that we all have more to learn in order to face up to conflict—latent or manifest—rather than avoid it, communicate constructively and effectively with others and enhance our capacity to learn from experience in managing conflict. Conflict management coaching helps us be effective in direct negotiations, mediation, informal processes and everyday life. Each of us makes mistakes, has buttons that can be pushed, areas of particular sensitivity. Conflict management coaching aims to expand our self-awareness and build our confidence to deal with conflict. Instead of leaving our response to conflict to chance, assuming that we will "muddle through," conflict management coaching accepts conflict as a reality in everyone's life and elevates our personal approaches to conflict to the level of learnable skills and achievable goals.

For many years, Cinnie Noble has been the go-to person for developing practical systems of conflict management coaching. Her wide-ranging experience in this area has led her to develop the CINERGY™ process—a powerful system for building on each of our natural skills as communicators and conflict intervenors to move into the role of conflict coach. CINERGY™ is built on three foundations, or pillars, as Cinnie refers to them—the knowledge, skills and insights of coaching, Alternative Dispute Resolution and neuroscience. From these three very different, but powerful bedrocks, Cinnie has found the synergies that propel CINERGY™.

Effective approaches to conflict intervention—and perhaps to all interventions into human relationships—have to operate on multiple levels. They must provide practical skills and tactics for helping people change how they understand the challenge before them, how they communicate and how they understand their own genuine needs and those of others. They also have to provide the conceptual tools that move us beyond a cookbook approach to intervention so that we can move in many directions, depending on who and what we are dealing with.

In this book, Cinnie moves us from the practical to the conceptual and back again, repeatedly and effectively. And what's more—it's a good read. We hope you will enjoy this journey into the world of conflict management coaching as much as we have.

Julie Macfarlane, PhD
Professor, University of Windsor
Windsor, Ontario

Bernie Mayer, PhD
Professor, the Werner Institute
Creighton University
Kingsville, Ontario

Acknowledgments

This book took a long time to come to fruition. Its completion date became a moving target and a subject of jokes among those who were about to take bets on when it would be complete! Where do I begin to thank everyone who supported me, who cheered me on and who contributed their ideas for this book?

First and foremost, I am beyond grateful for the dedication of my assistant, Laureen McNeill. Her care, thoughtfulness and patience kept me pushing forward on the days I felt daunted in my efforts to write my fifth and so far most challenging text.

The study group members and my clients are way up there on my gratitude list. Not only did they help inform the content of this book; it is from them that I learned most about the human experience of conflict. I thank them for their trust, for letting me know what I needed to learn and for keeping me humble, curious and in awe of the wonders of conflict. Similarly, I want to acknowledge and thank the thousands of people around the world who have taken the training and continue to contribute to the growing community of practice.

I deeply appreciate the caring, support and thoughtfulness of dear friends Jennifer Lynch, Deborah Katz and Carole Houk, for always being there in the many ways they are. That sentiment also extends to special friends Ann Begler, Brigida Colangelo, Christine Hart, Enid Lipsett, Frances Gregory, Christine Karcza, Sharron Kussiar, Kathy McLaughlin, Carol Myron, Lynne Raskin and Candace Seguinot.

How grateful I am to the incredible CINERGY™ trainers Lynora Brooke, Nicole Charron, Terry McCarthy, Janie Neff, Catherine O'Connell, Phil O'Hehir, Mary Lou O'Kennedy, Patricia Porter, Mary Rafferty, Heidi Ruppert, Rho Sandburg, Julie Walker and Leah Walls and coach-mentors Lucie Allaire, Lucille Boettger, Judy Felix, Ana

Gonçalves, Carole Grace, Berry Kruijning, Louise Page, John Roberts, Vanessa Toy, Sue Waterhouse and Susan Whillas. Their loyalty and commitment, and the ways in which they graciously pay forward their wisdom to those who participate in the training and to the individuals they coach, are truly wonderful. I similarly extend heartfelt thanks to CINERGY™ licensees LEADR (Fiona Hollier), CLE Consulting Australia (Rho Sandburg) and Convirgente (François Bogacz and Ana Gonçalves), working steadfastly behind the scenes to bring the workshops to many parts of the world.

My sincere gratefulness to special colleagues Julie Macfarlane, Bernie Mayer, Craig Runde (and members of the Advisory Board of the Center for Conflict Dynamics), Tammy Lenski, Paul Emond, Debra Dupree, Leslie MacLeod, Helen Marks, the team of coaches and staff of the Office of Collaborative Strategies at TSA, Tricia S. Jones and Ross Brinkert, Resa Eisen, Michael Rawlings, Stephanie West Allen, the members of the NextGen Leaders, the co-chairs and other leaders of the Workplace Section of the Association for Conflict Resolution and members of its Conflict Coaching Committee.

From the coaching field, my sincere appreciation to wonderful coaches Michael Bungay Stanier, Cynthia Calluori, Rey Carr, Ed Modell, Jeannie Nishimura, Linda Page, Pamela Richarde, Michael Rawlings, Merle Rockwell, Adria Trowhill, members of the International Coach Federation: Conflict Management Coaching Special Interest Group and the Conflict Coaching Guild on LinkedIn.

With many thanks to my tireless and thorough editor, Francine Geraci, and to Paula Pike, Jim Lyons and Tara Wells from WordsWorth Communications for your professionalism, creativity and care.

Last but by no means least, how grateful I am for the love and support of my devoted family—Honey and Gord, Jay, Allison and Adam, Tim, Shannon, Kye and Abi.

Cinnie Noble
September 2011

Introduction

In the last two to three decades, there has been exponential growth in two important fields of practice—coaching and Alternative Dispute Resolution (ADR). The specialty of conflict management coaching unites these two disciplines. Fast emerging as a coaching specialty and conflict management technique, this process has found a place within both. This chapter describes the genesis and development of the CINERGY™ model of conflict management coaching, as well as the step-by-step approach taken in this book.

The Development of Conflict Management Coaching

At the time I created the CINERGY™ model of conflict management coaching in the late 1990s, I had worked for many years as a lawyer-mediator. In this capacity, I assisted people to work through their interpersonal conflicts and saw the value of the mediation process within organizations and in other contexts. As an external contractor, I became increasingly aware over time of how many leaders and other staff in both private and public sector organizations demonstrated a

1

tendency to avoid conflict or to handle it in ways that did not serve them or others well. One of those ways—and a common pattern in managing interpersonal workplace disputes—is reactive, such that conflicts are not addressed until the situation becomes problematic or intolerable.

Like other Alternative Dispute Resolution (ADR) consultants and practitioners, I was most often called in after matters had escalated, after grievances and litigation had cost organizations financially, after staff had left or required prolonged medical or stress leave, after the workplace had become toxic, after productivity had suffered and after the organization's reputation had declined. Fractured relationships, ongoing infighting, increased tension and the other outcomes of poorly managed conflict prevail at these times, and beleaguered workplaces search for methods to improve things. It is evident, however, that when interpersonal conflict is not addressed or is left unresolved for too long, the health of the organization, work teams and the people directly and indirectly affected often suffer to the point that interventions are experienced as too little, too late. Benefits that could have been gained from the conflict and from early intervention are displaced by enormous financial and organizational stressors.

Some of the documented benefits of conflict include the fact that if effectively managed, conflict gives disputants opportunities to learn from one another, to collaborate, to improve their communication skills and relationships, to reconcile and accept differences, to gain new perspectives, and to develop creative and innovative solutions for handling issues in dispute and the contention that surrounds them. Generally speaking, however, it is not the norm in most workplaces that leaders and others invite and accept disparate viewpoints or engage in productive interactions regarding issues that challenge the status quo.

What became evident to me in my experience was that there were limited processes that offer people one-on-one assistance to gain the knowledge, skills and ability to engage in conflict in constructive and productive ways, to pre-empt unnecessary escalation, to regulate their emotions and to manage the impact of conflict on those who are directly and indirectly involved. This realization led to my research and to the development of a model that provides individualized and customized coaching to assist people in improving the way they engage in conflict, and to be able to do so independently.

Helping individuals with their interpersonal conflicts on a one-on-one basis is certainly not a new concept. Even without a specialized model, coaches regularly help their clients find their way through conflict. In the field of ADR, one of the many roles of organizational ombudsmen is to assist individual staff members. As well, human resource (HR) professionals, managers, supervisors, team leaders, lawyers, union representatives, counselors from employee assistance programs, therapists, psychologists and others help individuals with conflict in their lives. Many practitioners, however, are increasingly seeing the advantages of having a specific framework for providing conflict management coaching (or conflict coaching, as it is also called).

The definition of conflict management coaching used in this book is *a one-on-one process in which a trained coach helps people gain increased competence and confidence to manage and engage in interpersonal conflicts and disputes*. The text you are about to read describes the CINERGY™ model of conflict management coaching, and provides tools to support its practice.

Besides the play on my first name in the word CINERGY™, the dictionary definition of synergy is meaningful and relevant. Synergy is defined as *the cooperation of two or more things to produce a combined effect greater than the sum of their separate effects* (*Thesaurus of Current English*, 2007). This is what occurs between a specially trained coach and client who wishes to optimize his or her potential for effectively engaging in conflict. The synergy between the coach and the client has an impact not only on clients, but also on those around them who benefit from the increased learning and awareness that comes with skillful conflict management coaching. Synergy is what occurred, too, among members of a study group whom I involved in the development of the model, as you will read about next.

The Genesis of the CINERGY™ Model

When I began giving thought to what I viewed as a gap in the provision of an individualized approach to conflict management, I did not know of coaching models in either the ADR or coaching fields. In 1998 I read the article "Problem Solving for One,"[1] which described a process that was developed at McQuarrie University in Australia to assist university students when the other party in a dispute did not want to participate in (or did not show up for) mediation. The process reportedly helped individual students to explore their options and solutions.

Around the same time, I also contacted Ross Brinkert at Temple University, who was using a conflict-styles approach for coaching individual students when the other person in a dispute did not attend a mediation or one of the parties did not want to participate. He and Tricia S. Jones later went on to develop the Comprehensive Conflict Coaching Model and, in 2008, published the first book on the subject of conflict coaching.[2] However, finding no specific training or models of the nature I envisioned when I was exploring the concept of one-on-one work, I decided to become certified as a coach and to explore developing a conflict management coaching model. Early in my studies, I saw another synergy—one between the professions of coaching and mediation.

To experiment and study what would constitute a model of this nature, I initially brought together 12 people from a range of backgrounds. I refer to them and the additional people who were involved in the pilot stage of the CINERGY™ model as the study group members. I inquired, from a number of private and public sector workplaces for which I had provided mediation, whether I might recruit volunteers from a cross-section of their staff who were willing to devote some time to work on challenges with interpersonal workplace disputes and improve their conflict competence. From the overwhelming response I received, I could have started with many, many more! However, I chose to begin with a small group. Later, I returned to these organizations to request additional volunteers to test the model.

The first steps with the initial study group members involved working with each person individually for one hour a week, for a six-week period. During this time, I walked them through a basic coaching framework, which involved assisting each person to identify his or her conflict management goals, to explore different perspectives on their disputes, to brainstorm and select the possibilities for the way forward, to take active steps for reaching the optimal choice and to consider challenges that might arise in doing so. In developing a conflict management coaching model based on these components, and from other principles from the fields of coaching and conflict management discussed further in Chapter 1, I quickly realized that the part that required the most in-depth work had to do with how best to help people gain different perspectives on their conflicts and disputes.

Experiential Research

Albert Einstein had a well-known theory that problems cannot be solved by the level of awareness, thinking and consciousness that created them.[3] This theory resonated with me, and I began the journey to figure out a way to help people gain increased self-awareness and be able to reappraise themselves, their situations and the other people in their disputes.

How does someone gain a different perspective on his or her situation? I began the process with a close examination of three previous or current conflicts for each study group member. One thing that became evident was that the members followed certain patterns in how they processed their interactions—emotionally, intellectually and otherwise. I then applied this valuable information by further analyzing three conflict situations each for 40 more people. In the end, this experiential research informed the development of the stages of the CINERGY™ model, including a major part of the model that helps clients gain different perspectives by increasing their understanding of what happened for them and for the other person in their interaction. (These findings are discussed in Chapter 2.)

Through a staged approach that incrementally built on their awareness, study group members were able to reach their specific goals and discover improved ways of engaging in and managing their interpersonal disputes. This process, and the framework for coaching people through conflict that evolved, was tested and refined in 1999–2000 through individual and group work. It is evident from its use and training worldwide that the model works across cultures, in all types of workplaces and age groups, for both genders, for those at all levels of organizations and in a wide range of contexts.

Integration Within a Conflict Management System

From early on, both public and private sector organizations and individual practitioners in Canada, the United States, Australia, Ireland and other parts of Europe began to incorporate the CINERGY™ model as another tool in their coaching and ADR services. For instance, this method is widely used in many informal conflict management systems throughout Canada's federal government.

In 2004, I was retained as a consultant to work with the Office of Collaborative Strategies of the US Transportation Security Administration (TSA), Homeland Security, to develop a conflict management coaching program with its internal program officer. Initially a peer coaching program, this was the first known endeavor to form part of what is known as an Integrated Conflict Management System. (More on the inclusion of conflict management coaching within organizational systems is discussed in Chapter 6.)

The Reasons for the Growth of Conflict Management Coaching

As a pioneer in the emergence of conflict management coaching, I have contemplated reasons for its growth. Here are some:

- Interpersonal disputes are inevitable, and the economic and human costs of poorly managed conflict are high. As a result, there is a need for more and different ways to help people strengthen this aspect of their lives.

- Organizations have limited individualized methods for helping people manage their disputes independently.

- Since the 1990s, professional coaching has been more and more accepted as a forum of choice for assisting individuals and groups to make changes in their personal and professional lives. As specialties continue to develop within this field, a niche such as conflict management coaching has a place within organizational, leadership, life and other forms of coaching.

- The concept of building conflict-competent organizations is growing. Along with this evolution, effective conflict management is identified as a core competency for leaders and others. One way to provide staff with ways to strengthen their knowledge, skills and abilities is through a customized process such as coaching to assist them on a one-on-one basis with their specific areas of development.

- Coaching is different from counseling and other therapeutic interventions that help individuals manage conflict. It offers a short-term, future-focused and defined goal-oriented process that helps people improve the way they engage in conflict.

- ADR professionals who provide conflict management services and training recognize the need for more ways to assist people to engage in conflict. For instance, conflict management coaching supports and prepares disputants to engage actively and effectively in ADR processes such as mediation, collaborative law, restorative justice, facilitated dialogues and so on.

The Intention of This Book

When I began to develop the CINERGY™ model, I envisioned a two-pronged process. One prong pertains to coaching individuals whose goals focus on increasing their conflict competence. In these cases, clients do not have one particular dispute in mind. Rather, they recognize that they do not engage effectively in conflict in general. They may exacerbate unnecessary disputes or respond in unproductive ways to people who provoke them, and they strive to learn constructive methods for interacting and communicating. The other prong in the CINERGY™ approach pertains to coaching individuals who want to gain skills and confidence to independently manage or resolve a specific dispute, or to prepare for an anticipated one.

The intention of this book is to share the framework that applies to both prongs. Over the 12 years since I developed the CINERGY™ model, I and others have found many applications, and some are detailed in Chapter 6.

Another intention of my writing this book is to provide readers with suggestions regarding the practice of conflict management coaching—to share lessons that I have learned that may help others who are developing their coaching practice or who are adding conflict management coaching to their current services. I also thought it would be helpful to provide real-life examples. With the permission of my clients, most of the scenarios in this book are based on actual situations (though changes have been made to remove any possible identification). Any similarities to readers' experiences are coincidental.

A challenge in writing this book was to decide which audiences to speak to. Conflict management coaching straddles several fields of practice, including my chosen professions of coaching and mediation.

Over the years, the CINERGY™ model has drawn coaches, mediators and others from the ADR field. I knew from my own training that coaches would know the fundamentals of coaching, the requisite skills and the logistical components. I also found that, generally speaking, many members of this audience do not have a conflict management background. By the same token, mediators and other conflict management practitioners have the knowledge and experience of working with people in conflict, though many have not yet learned coaching principles and practices. In addition, HR professionals, leaders, lawyers, psychologists, social workers and union representatives participate in conflict management coaching training. They bring a wide range of other related experiences from their roles, as do academics and students of coaching, conflict management and law.

To decide on content that had broad appeal, I consulted CINERGY™ trainers and coach-mentors and considered comments and questions from thousands of workshop participants with these varied backgrounds. In the end, I drew from the input of this entire range of people to impart what I hope will fill gaps in the knowledge that readers currently have.

How This Book Is Organized

Chapter 1 defines conflict management coaching and provides the specific theory, principles and practices from the fields of both coaching and conflict management that inform the CINERGY™ model. The model is also grounded in neuroscience principles, a number of which are included in the chapter. From this starting point, readers will become more aware of how concepts from these various fields are integrated within the coaching process.

Chapter 2 begins the discussion on analyzing conflict by first developing the concept of conflict habits. How these are embedded from many influences in our lives, and become the rules we live by regarding the ways we and others "should" behave, are considered. This chapter also presents a way for clients to break down a conflict by exploring the various elements that led to its evolution. The analysis and the resulting construct, termed the (Not So) Merry-Go-Round of Conflict, are based on the aforementioned research in the development of the CINERGY™ model, about ways to help people gain different perspectives. Chapter 2 also discusses emotions, a critical component of conflict.

With this theoretical base, Chapter 3 goes on to provide a number of practical and logistical considerations. The chapter covers the inquiry and intake stages of conflict management coaching, and also deals with frequently asked questions. The intake stage provides information and forms that may be used once the client agrees to proceed with coaching.

Chapter 4 outlines the CINERGY™ model of conflict management coaching. The intent of each of the seven stages is provided, along with commentary and considerations for conducting each step.

Chapter 5 describes a number of coaching skills and gives examples of their application. Because ethics is considered an aspect of the skill base required to be a masterful coach, this chapter also provides a suggested model for standards of ethical conduct for conflict management coaches.

Chapter 6 explains a number of applications of conflict management coaching that have evolved over time. One of the most popular applications has been in the field of mediation. This chapter elaborates on using conflict management coaching in a pre- and post-mediation forum, as well as during the process.

Chapter 7, the final chapter, presents a range of ways for measuring the effectiveness of conflict management coaching. Variables such as return on investment, clients' success, and satisfaction with the coach and with the process are discussed. Pertinent questionnaires are also provided. The chapter includes several assessment tools specific to evaluating conflict behaviors and styles, as well as some ideas for future research relating to conflict management coaching.

Notes

1. A. Tidwell, "Problem Solving for One," *Mediation Quarterly* 14 (1997): 304–17.

2. Tricia S. Jones and Ross Brinkert, *Conflict Coaching: Conflict Management Strategies for the Individual* (Los Angeles: Sage, 2008).

3. Albert Einstein, *Ideas and Opinions* (New York: Three Rivers Press, 1954).

CHAPTER 1

The Three Pillars of Conflict Management Coaching

You will have read in the Introduction about the initial development of the CINERGY™ model and the intention behind it, which was to build its framework on the principles and practice of coaching and conflict management. With my feet firmly planted in both these fields as a certified coach and mediator, it seemed a natural fit—and it was. However, I was not aware, in the early stages, of how studies in neuroscience would contribute to the model's effectiveness. This chapter describes how principles from these three pillars support and inform the theoretical and practical base used in this model for coaching individuals through their interpersonal conflicts and disputes.

What Is Conflict Management Coaching?

As defined in the Introduction, conflict management coaching, also known as conflict coaching, is a one-on-one process in which a trained coach helps individuals gain increased competence and confidence to manage and engage in their interpersonal conflicts and disputes. It is a goal-oriented and future-focused process that concentrates on assisting clients to reach their specific conflict management objectives. There are many reasons that people seek, or are referred to, conflict management coaching. Some real-life examples follow.

> Manny and Cleo have worked on the same team for two years, and they constantly disagree on various aspects of joint projects. Manny, who wants to apply to be a Team Leader, realizes he needs to figure out better ways of working with Cleo and to manage conflict more effectively, in general. He acknowledges a tendency to become defensive when anyone disputes his ideas, and he wants to be more adept at engaging with co-workers when differences of opinion arise.

> One of the things Hilda hates about her new job as a manager is performance reviews. There are two staff members whom she finds combative at the best of times. Whenever she gives them feedback, Hilda expects a backlash. She went to a course recently on performance management, and though she learned a lot of theory and practiced role plays, Hilda wants more help with her specific challenges and her general fear of conflict.

Khalid and Jenna attended a mediation a few weeks ago regarding several issues that they were unable to resolve together in their work unit. They seemed to come to agreement about those matters. However, the two have not spoken since. Jenna acknowledges that she resents Khalid for initiating the mediation, and believes she did not handle herself as well as she could have. She knows she is generally not resilient when it comes to conflict. Jenna wants to overcome this trait and also apologize to Khalid for some things she said. She prefers to do so without involving anyone else.

Whether or not clients' conflicts are workplace-related, their goals in coaching fall under several general themes:

- To explore what, if anything, to do about a dispute that has already occurred.
- To consider the most appropriate strategies and approaches in managing a conflict that is currently in progress.
- To prepare for a one-on-one interaction, for example, a performance review, disciplinary conversation or other situation that is expected to be challenging.
- To consider how to approach a situation that could escalate into an unnecessary argument.
- To prepare for presenting a topic to a group that is likely to engender adverse reactions.
- To talk out thoughts and feelings about a fractious situation.
- To examine the choices and solutions that may be feasible for resolving issues that are in dispute.
- To prepare for mediation or another process such as negotiation, arbitration, restorative justice, collaborative law or group facilitation.

The stages of the CINERGY™ model and how it helps clients achieve goals such as these are described in Chapter 4. The theoretical and practical underpinnings that ground the model's philosophy and operation are described below.

The Pillar of Coaching

The first use of the word "coaching" in the organizational context goes back to 1937.[1] Since that time, much research and many books and articles have documented the evolution of this field. Coaching has a rich heritage based on the theory and principles of many areas of study and practice, including adult learning, psychotherapy, the self-help movement, leadership, social systems, Eastern philosophy, hope theory, communications, training, change and risk management, neuroscience, psychology and appreciative inquiry. There are different types of coaching, such as executive/leadership, organizational, business and life coaching, and many sub-specialties, of which conflict management coaching is one.

Coaching is a field that has steadily grown as a method for helping people who are striving to optimize their potential. It is rooted in the premise that we have the ability to reach goals beyond our current measure of achievement. Coaching helps people stretch themselves in different ways to reach objectives that enhance and give new direction and meaning to their personal and professional lives. It is a practice that operates on the basis that people who seek or are referred to coaching have the ability to access the information, knowledge, resources and wisdom to make changes, to choose different actions and to shift habits that are not working for them.

There are many definitions of coaching. The following extracts are from the International Coach Federation (ICF):

> Coaching is partnering with clients in a thought-provoking and creative process that inspires them to maximize their personal and professional potential.[2]

> Coaching is an ongoing relationship which focuses on clients taking action toward the realization of their visions, goals or desires.[3]

Coaching is a transformative process for personal and professional awareness, discovery and growth.[4]

The Association for Coaching (AC), another international organization, defines coaching as

[a] collaborative solution-focused, results-oriented and systematic process in which the coach facilitates the enhancement of work performance, life experience, self-directed learning and personal growth of the coachee.[5]

How Does Coaching Work?

Coaching is a results-oriented process that helps clients work through any challenges to achieving change, including their self-limiting beliefs. To perform the coaching role effectively, coaches create a nurturing and safe environment. Together with each client, they co-create the coaching relationship.

Coaches follow either a specific or a general model that guides the process, aimed at moving clients along a continuum from where they are to where they want to be. This is done by way of an informal dialogue within which coaches ask clients strategic questions aimed at increasing their self-awareness. Coaches acknowledge clients' situations, provide observations and challenge them to move out of their comfort zones to reach their goals. They offer clients inspiration, motivation, support and feedback to facilitate their success. They also stay attuned to whether clients are remaining accountable to expend the time, energy and effort needed to progress and reach their objectives.

Many professional coaches, including those trained in the CINERGY™ model, do not provide clients with strategies, advice or opinions. Rather, they help them tap into their own inner resources and intuition, trusting that clients are the authority on their decisions and are responsible for their own actions. The philosophy of the International Coach Federation resonates with the CINERGY™ model:

Coaching honors the client as the expert in his/her life and work and believes that every client is creative, resourceful, and whole. Standing on this foundation, the coach's responsibility is to:

- Discover, clarify, and align with what the client wants to achieve;
- Encourage client self-discovery;
- Elicit client-generated solutions and strategies; and
- Hold the client responsible and accountable.[6]

Why Does Coaching Work?

Coaching works for many reasons:

- Coaches honor self-determination as a fundamental principle. This increases clients' abilities to explore their own instincts, insights and wisdom, and is inspiring and motivating for people who aim to make changes in their lives.
- Coaching requires a collaborative and purposeful relationship. This in and of itself inspires clients to experience that their journey is not a solitary one. Knowing that someone is supporting them along the way is energizing and comforting for clients.
- The synergy that develops between the coach and client as the relationship gains trust and strength creates positive energy and optimism, increasing clients' creativity and motivation.
- As new and different realizations emerge, clients gain momentum. These insights and learnings inspire even more expansive thinking.
- Being accountable for their own progress stretches clients to do the requisite work to reach their goals.

Although coaching is becoming increasingly well known, people still often ask how it compares with other human services, such as consulting, mentoring, psychotherapy and counseling. Readers who want more information on how these services compare can refer to Appendix I.

Further principles from the field of coaching that informed the development of the CINERGY™ model include the following:

- Coaches focus on strengths rather than weaknesses—on the positive and not the negative.
- Coaches are facilitative change agents who serve their clients' positive interests.
- Coaches remain aware of clients' individual cultures, contexts and environments, and work within these.

The Pillar of Alternative Dispute Resolution

The second pillar of the CINERGY™ model derives from Alternative Dispute Resolution (ADR), specifically, the technique of mediation. Mediation is a process in which an impartial facilitator (the mediator) manages the discussions and negotiations between or among two or more people. Depending on the type of mediation and the orientation of the mediator, the practitioner's role is to help disputants resolve their issues, reconcile the breakdown of their relationship or reach other outcomes that the parties identify.

Over the past 30 years, mediation has steadily emerged as a useful and conciliatory mechanism in a range of contexts. The techniques in this field evolved from, among other things, a need to find more expedient, less costly and more collaborative ways to help people re-solve their disputes other than through the courts (in other words, an "alternative" to legal proceedings). The acronym ADR has also been defined as "Appropriate" Dispute Resolution. That is, disputing parties may choose, from among a range of possible methods, the one or ones suitable for them and their conflict situation.

Other ADR mechanisms include group facilitation, conciliation, ombudsmen, restorative justice processes, peer review panels, arbitration and collaborative law. Conflict management coaching is a relatively new addition to the wide spectrum of techniques in the ADR field.

Three more real-life scenarios further distinguish mediation and conflict management coaching. In these situations, the people involved may benefit from coaching, mediation or both. Chapter 6 explains how these processes may be done separately or in tandem.

> Karen was promoted to a management position six months ago. In the past month, three staff members complained to her boss Ted, saying Karen's micromanagement style was stifling them and that she argues with them when they ask for more voice on a number of matters. Ted conveyed this information to Karen, who reacted strongly, pointing out various bad habits that her staff members demonstrate, requiring her to "manage them tightly." A disagreement with Ted on the topic of management styles ensued. Karen left the meeting in a huff, and is now concerned that her response to her boss was career-limiting.

> George and Luis are co-workers who have not gotten along well since they began working together a year ago. Communication between them has been deteriorating over the past few weeks, and George realizes that the tension is having a huge impact on him. He now dreads going to work. George shared his concerns with two co-workers whom he trusts. One co-worker suggested mediation. The other suggested George see a conflict management coach.

Both Brian and Janice asked to be the lead on their company's new project, and their boss decided to appoint them as co-leaders. This situation has resulted in much tension between them. Initially, Janice and Brian both made an effort to work out their differences to help the project succeed. However, they are now openly arguing, and their colleagues are beginning to take sides. Janice is ignoring Brian, who does not want to go to the boss about this situation.

Which method should these disputants choose—conflict management coaching or mediation?

Coaches reading the above scenarios are likely to consider the advantages of individual coaching; mediators will likely suggest that mediation would provide a forum for both parties to resolve their differences together.

Either of these two methods—mediation or coaching—may be a viable option in the above scenarios. However, Karen may not like the idea of having a mediator assist her and her boss, and neither may her boss. Karen may prefer coaching on how to initiate and structure a conversation with Ted to rectify matters between them. She may also want to work on regulating her emotions, which typically escalate to her detriment when she perceives she is being criticized. Additionally, she may want some coaching on how to improve her management style to avoid similar problems with her staff in the future.

George may want the opportunity to talk with a coach to figure out what is happening between him and Luis. He may decide to continue with coaching if he wants to manage the situation himself. On the other hand, he might like the idea of their manager or a mediator facilitating a dialogue between them.

Brian may seek individual assistance to consider the best approach for improving communication between Janice and himself. Because he does not want to involve their boss, coaching may suit him more.

When two people are aware there is a dispute between them and they are both willing to resolve things together with the assistance of a third party, mediation is a useful technique that is offered in many workplaces and other contexts. However, coaching may be preferred in the following circumstances:

- One or more of the disputants wants to gain the knowledge, skills and ability to manage situations by him- or herself.
- One or both of the disputants does not want to have a third party involved.
- Animosity between the parties is high and there is limited, if any, willingness to work together.
- The parties have disparate objectives regarding the outcome of mediation, which may frustrate or even exacerbate matters.
- One or both of the disputants is embarrassed or ashamed about the conflict and does not want to engage in a process that may make others in the organization aware of the discord—for instance, the manager, the person or department that coordinates the mediation, and so on.
- Although mediation is meant to be informal, it is not always experienced as such. In a workplace dispute, some clients may consider mediation a more formal process than is necessary for what they want to achieve. Others do not want minutes of settlement or a filing of any sort with their manager in their personnel records (if it is the organization's practice to keep related records in employees' files).
- Mediation is premised on the parties' voluntary participation, but some people may perceive that their attendance is mandatory. Any related resistance adds another layer to the conflict dynamic.
- One party is concerned that raising and resolving issues in mediation will create retaliatory and other negative outcomes.
- One disputant resists facing a manager or another staff member in a higher position where a power imbalance exists

between the parties. Similarly, an employee may consider that initiating mediation with a manager or other authority figure would be inappropriate, for cultural or other reasons.

Experienced mediators work through many of the above circumstances on a regular basis. However, when given the choice, some people consider conflict management coaching to be a more appropriate process for what they wish to achieve. Readers wanting more information about the differences and similarities between mediation and conflict management coaching may refer to Appendix II. Chapter 6 will discuss how these two processes may work together.

Different Types of Mediation

There are many different forms of mediation. Principles from five of them, described below, are relevant to the CINERGY™ model.

Interest-Based Mediation

The approach of interest-based negotiation and mediation is primarily problem-solving. The mediator's role is to foster a cooperative forum and help the disputants achieve resolution of their issues. The practitioner engages the parties to identify and explore what it is they want, to generate options and, generally, to discuss settlement terms that meet mutually acceptable objective criteria. Though the CINERGY™ model is least connected to the principles of this approach, several concepts from this type of mediation have some relevance and are briefly summarized here. They are based on Roger Fisher's and William Ury's book *Getting to Yes: Negotiating Agreement Without Giving In*[7]:

- In the course of mediation, the facilitator asks the parties to identify what they want as a resolution. This outcome represents their *positions*. The facilitator then takes the disputants' stated positions further by having them focus on why they are important for them. This approach helps the parties identify their hopes, expectations and underlying needs, which represent their *interests*. Interest-based mediation aims at uncovering the motivating force behind disputants' stated positions. The theory and practice here is that parties are better able to brainstorm a range of settlement options that are complementary and will advance their respective interests.

- People typically mediate and negotiate their differences with the intention of producing better results than they might otherwise obtain. If they are unaware of the results they risk through unsuccessful negotiations, they may enter into an agreement that they would be better off rejecting. On the other hand, they may reject an agreement that they would be better off accepting. This component of the interest-based process supports the idea that disputants consider their best alternative if negotiations break down before rejecting or accepting a resolution. The acronym BATNA (Best Alternative To a Negotiated Agreement) derives from this principle.

The CINERGY™ model does not necessarily aim at resolving the client's differences with another, as settlement of specific issues may not be the objective for seeking coaching. In fact, a client's desired outcome may not be compatible with what the other person wants. For instance, a person's objective in coaching may be to gain assistance in initiating a conversation with a friend with whom he or she is always in conflict about ending their relationship. The model does, however, help individuals explore what is important to them with respect to what they want to achieve and why. It also assists clients to consider their options for reaching their desired outcomes. The above components, and others relating to interest-based processes, also have a place in the coaching model when clients are exploring issues in preparation for mediation, negotiation or other ADR techniques.

Transformative Mediation

Concepts from Transformative Mediation referred to here are from books by Robert A. Baruch Bush and Joseph P. Folger—*The Promise of Mediation: Responding to Conflict Through Empowerment and Recognition* and *The Promise of Mediation: The Transformative Approach to Conflict*.[8] The following paragraph, from the latter text, reflects the basic theory of Transformative Mediation, which is also inherent in the CINERGY™ model:

> This transformational potential stems from mediation's capacity to generate two important effects, empowerment and recognition. In simplest terms, *empowerment* means the restoration to individuals of a sense of their own value and strength and their own capacity to handle life's problems. *Recognition* means the evocation in individuals of acknowledgement and empathy for the situation and problems of others. When both of these processes are held central in the practice of mediation, parties are helped to use conflicts as opportunities for moral growth, and the transformational potential of mediation is realized.[9]

Here are some further principles from the transformative framework of Bush and Folger that also apply in the CINERGY™ model:

- Human beings are fundamentally social and desire constructive interaction. (This point of view underpins *social constructionism*, a sociological theory of knowledge.)
- Conflict represents a relational crisis that destabilizes people. As a result, they act and interact in ways that produce unproductive and destructive dynamics.
- People in conflict have the capacity to change the quality of their interactions and regenerate their relationships and communication, in constructive ways.
- It is up to the people in conflict to identify and clarify their goals. The outcomes are also their responsibility.

- Facilitators take an optimistic view of the disputants' motives and competence.
- Facilitators are responsive to the emotional expression of people in conflict.
- Exploring the parties' uncertainties ultimately helps them to dispel their confusion.

Though not all concepts from the Transformative Mediation framework are applicable to the CINERGY™ model, the above points illustrate a number of shared philosophical and practical underpinnings.

Narrative Mediation

The principles that follow are based on the book *Narrative Mediation: A New Approach to Conflict Resolution* by John Winslade and Gerald Monk.[10] This approach, like the transformative process just described, also has its roots in social constructionism and similarly departs from the traditional interest-based approaches for resolving disputes.

Narrative Mediation facilitators encourage disputants to gain understanding about their conflicts through discovering their shared social and cultural narratives. This form of mediation concentrates on the importance of building a new story of the disputing parties' relationship that is not compatible with their conflict stories. Some principles from the Narrative Mediation framework that are relevant to the CINERGY™ model follow:

- The facts of the stories that each person brings to the forum are not the focus.
- Strategic questioning serves to probe the deeper meaning expressed by the disputants. By increasing their knowledge, the parties have the opportunity to re-evaluate their initial perspectives and explore other possibilities.
- Deconstructing and reconstructing conflict situations are integral steps for assisting people in re-scripting their conflict stories.
- Gaining perspective on the other person's viewpoint is integral to the process.

Insight Mediation

Another approach to discussing differences with the help of a third-party facilitator is Insight Mediation, described in the book *Transforming Conflict Through Insight* by Kenneth R. Melchin and Cheryl A. Picard.[11] Insight Mediation is not so much focused on resolution as it is on ensuring that the parties "engage in fair and fruitful conversations."[12] The theory and practice reflect the view that value narratives from our past give rise to feelings of threat that distort our understanding of others. Those who practice this form of mediation invite disputing parties to understand why this is so and to examine deeper levels of their values and feelings.[13] Facilitators also help the parties de-link the perception that the other person's cares and concerns are necessarily a threat to their own.

Here are some other points from the insight approach that relate to the CINERGY™ model:

- We are social beings and seek to understand ourselves and others in relation to the traditions and various influences that shape us.
- Our actions arise from our beliefs about how people should engage with others.
- Insights into our values, cares and related threats have the potential to shift the way we think and feel about our values and the other person's. Such shifts change how we view our conflicts.

Solution-Focused Conflict Management

This type of conflict management process, as described by Fredrike Bannink in her *Handbook of Solution-Focused Conflict Management*,[14] has its roots in solution-focused grief therapy. Several basic principles in this practice also resound with the CINERGY™ model. These include not dwelling extensively on past problems but rather, helping clients investigate new forward-thinking possibilities. Like facilitators of solution-focused processes, conflict management coaches develop effective questioning skills to help clients explore their feelings and gain insights and increased awareness.

Other concepts that share the premises of the CINERGY™ model include the following:

- Clients are the experts on themselves.
- Clients are able to move forward when they identify their previous successes, including the ability to make changes and recognize what is already working.
- Clients are expected to be accountable to take action.
- Understanding and acknowledging the other person's perspective is an important aspect of reconciling differences.
- Individualized goals, and the clients' definition of success in reaching them, are pivotal for measuring progress.
- Small, incremental changes are signs of progress.

These brief descriptions of principles from various approaches to mediation and ADR reflect some aspects of the CINERGY™ model of conflict management coaching. The methodology behind its framework that emerged in the experiential study I conducted of the evolution of group members' conflicts and disputes is also supported by recent research into the human brain. Some findings from this research form the third pillar, to be discussed next.

The Pillar of Neuroscience

In an interdisciplinary field such as coaching—which, among other things, is about people making changes in their lives—coaches are learning a great deal from the advances in research relating to the brain. Similarly, the ADR field has taken an interest in how neural activity has an impact on emotions, decision-making, creativity and so on.

The concept of interpersonal biology, as described by Daniel Siegel,[15] joins cognitive neuroscience with psychotherapy and reflects a focus on brain function and structure that develop within the body and in relation to other people. Social cognitive neuroscience[16] integrates areas of research traditionally within the purview of social psychology, such as attitude change and emotional regulation. However, it uses methods usually employed by cognitive neuroscientists, including functional brain imaging and neuropsychological analysis.

This part of the chapter considers findings from these areas of study that are relevant to the CINERGY™ model. The references here merely touch upon the extensive research and work of many scientists, academics and others who are expanding our knowledge about how we can change our lives by better understanding our brains.

Focusing Attention

> Focusing attention facilitates new thinking.

One recent and highly significant discovery is that concentrated attention and intention help to form new neural pathways that can change the way we think and feel. *Neuroplasticity* refers to the property of the brain that allows it to change itself. It springs from the root words "neuro" for neurons (the nerve cells in the brain) and "plastic" in the sense of being able to change and adapt. According to research, people must first increase the "attention density" in specific circuits of their brain before they can alter their patterns of thinking. Attention density refers to the quality and quantity of the focus paid—a focus that brings into play the Quantum Zeno Effect, described as follows:

> This [attention density] is a basic principle of quantum physics—the rate of observation has marked measurable effects on the phenomenon being observed. The Quantum Zeno Effect for neuroscience application states that the mental act of focusing attention holds in place brain circuits associated with

what is being focused on. If you pay enough attention to a certain set of brain connections, it keeps this relevant circuitry stable, open and dynamically alive, enabling it to eventually becoming a part of the brain's hard wiring.[17]

In this regard, psychiatrist Jeffrey M. Schwartz states, "The power is in the focus. Where we choose to put our attention changes our brain and changes how we interact with the world."[18] He and others who have studied this concept have found that with enough attention density—which requires repetition, focus and time—we ultimately manifest what is needed to make the desired changes. We gain new thoughts about what it is we intend to do, and these become part of our neural circuitry, resulting in different ways of perceiving our worlds. This phenomenon is known as self-directed neuroplasticity.

Based on related research, David Rock, a leader in the field of human performance coaching, elaborates on this concept in his book *Your Brain at Work*: "Looking out for your goal, you are more likely to perceive information relating to it, which makes you feel positive, because you feel that the goal is going to happen, which makes you look out for it more, and perceive more information, and so on."[19]

The implications for coaches working with clients who want to make changes in their lives is evident. Among other things, the coach's task is to keep clients focused on their goals and intentions. Asking clients to name their objectives and intentions not only gives them a sense of purpose. It also provides a focus for them and for the coach to facilitate self-directed neuroplasticity and measure progress and change. The importance, then, of staying focused on goals and working toward them in a disciplined way cannot be overstated.

Further in this regard, if clients in conflict management coaching concentrate on what went wrong rather than looking ahead with fresh thinking, they stand to remain entrenched in a problem-saturated mindset. Similarly, clients who lose their focus owing to internal or external distractions, or who act contrary to their stated objective, can lose the requisite attention density and reinforce old or alternative patterns.[20]

"Toward" Goals

> "Toward" goals inspire forward movement.

A significant principle related to attention and intention is helping clients to reach their objectives through "toward" goals. These are the objectives on which clients focus their energies and seek to create new, positive connections. Toward goals inspire the state of being curious, open and interested, attitudes that are necessary for change, learning, insight and creativity. There is inherent optimism in setting goals. And when clients begin to take small steps to reach them, they typically experience more clarity, a sense of accomplishment and enhanced positivity.

In contrast, "away" goals might include considering what could go wrong, a focus that activates negative emotions such as fear, anxiety and uncertainty and can lead to avoidance.[21] According to Rock, "The trouble is, because problems come to mind so much easier than solutions, people tend to set 'away goals,' and since problems are more certain than unknown solutions, the brain naturally steers toward certainty."[22]

Goal-setting works best if clients name their own objectives and coaches support them to maintain their purpose and intention as "toward" goals.

Helping Clients Gain Insights

> Coaches help their clients gain insights into themselves and the conflict dynamic.

Insights are those moments of clarity when something suddenly makes sense. It has been said that "[a]n insight is a restructuring of information—it's seeing the same old thing in a completely new way."[23]

Through strategic questioning and use of other skills, coaches help clients to gain insights and self-awareness, qualities that improve their "mental maps"—how they perceive the world and feel about the issues they are working on.

What leads clients to insights into their habitual patterns? This topic is of great interest to coaches, who recognize that the experience of expanded awareness inspires, excites and energizes clients to think and feel differently about the issues they are exploring. New insights and perspectives open up new possibilities, choices and opportunities. But "people ... experience the adrenaline-like rush of insight only if they go through the process of making connections themselves."[24]

Author Jonah Lehrer refers to several other key features of insights. Insights are typically preceded by an impasse or block. This is evident in coaching when clients are still engaged in old ways of thinking and feeling and are not yet ready or open to new ones. Another key feature of insight is that when a breakthrough occurs, people seem to move instantaneously from impasse to "aha!" like a revelation, with an accompanying feeling of certainty.[25]

Studies reveal that although insights appear to come out of nowhere, the brain is usually preparing itself for a new awareness. Cognitive neuroscientists Mark Jung-Beeman and John Kounios, who have individually and together conducted a great deal of research on this subject, discovered that the insight process is an act of "cognitive deliberation." After the first "preparatory phase," the brain begins looking for answers (the "search phase"), during which period the cortex needs to relax ("relaxation phase"). At these times, it is important to let the mind wander to be able to reflect and tap into the part of the brain from where the insight comes (the right hemisphere).[26]

The idea of focusing, yet also letting the mind wander, is supported by related research by Jonathan Schooler and others who study decision science.[27] In practice, it is evident that clients often come to new awareness between sessions when the seeds planted during the coaching conversation germinate once their brains relax and their minds wander. Similarly, when coaches quiet the space during coaching sessions by silently listening, clients' epiphanies often emerge as they contemplate a question and think and feel their thoughts and emotions.

Other related research from the fields of emotional intelligence and positive psychology has found that a positive mood stimulates optimism and increases ability to make decisions and solve problems with insight, compared with people in negative moods. Among other things, these findings support the importance of coaches' engendering optimism by creating a positive working relationship with clients and using mindfulness and other techniques to help quiet clients' minds and help them focus.[28]

Mindful Awareness

> Mindful awareness improves the capacity to regulate emotions, enhance patterns of thinking and reduce negativity.

Mindfulness refers to being aware in the moment of what we are experiencing. It has been described as "an experience rather than a precisely defined abstract construct," the key outcomes being "awareness of the present, non-judgment and acceptance."[29] Mindfulness has also been characterized as "dispassionate, non-evaluative and sustained moment to moment awareness of perceptible mental strategy and process"[30] and as comprising three elements: attention, purpose and non-judgment.[31] Another definition refers to mindfulness as "the state of awareness in which we are conscious of our feelings, thoughts and habits of mind and able to let unhelpful ones go so that they no longer limit us."[32] Social psychologist Ellen Langer contrasts mindfulness to the mindless state, in which we have rigid perspectives. In a mindful state, one constantly creates new categories, welcomes new information and is open to different points of view or perspectives.[33] All these and many other descriptions of mindfulness are relevant to helping clients develop a reflective mind that enables them to focus and to make their way through their conflicts.

One of the reported ways to embed new neural circuits is through mindful meditation. According to neuropsychologist Marsha Lucas, when we practice meditation, we notice our thoughts but do not let them get "tangled up." Rather, our brains "get better at making sense of incoming emotional information without jumping to conclusions, reacting out of old habits, or getting stuck in emotional dead-ends like worry or grudges. It does the right stuff with that incoming information, helping you to wisely tell the difference between what's happening in the moment, and what's your 'old stuff' pulling your strings like some predictable marionette." Lucas adds that "[y]our better-wired brain can then allow you to perceive and respond to others in balanced, mindful ways that support solid, healthy relationships."[34]

Also significant for coaches in this regard is the work of Daniel Siegel, author of *The Mindful Brain: Reflection and Attunement in the Cultivation of Well Being*. Siegel describes this form of mindful awareness as a way of enabling us to develop an attuned relationship with ourselves and with others.[35] He explains the concept of "attunement" as focusing our attention on another and on our relationship with that person so that we can "harness neural circuitry that enables two people 'to feel felt' by each other."[36]

To help clients become attuned this way is an integral part of coaching people through conflict. New awareness often evolves for clients when coaches help them to bring some objectivity to their situation and notice the nature of their thoughts and feelings.

Similar to the notion of mindfulness and the idea of observing what is going on without being attached to it, coaches work with clients to facilitate their ability to articulate the current reality of their thinking, and also to step back and think about their thinking. This approach gives people the opportunity to consider what is happening for them in less reactive and more reflective ways.

With concentrated effort, then, there is significant potential for facilitating the development of new, neural circuitry and for self-correcting old habits. How mindfulness techniques may be integrated into coaching is an ongoing dialogue among coaches and others who incorporate them into their practices and their own self-work.

Harnessing Clients' Creativity

> Coaches help clients harness their creativity to be able to act upon their new insights.

Coaches apply a variety of techniques to help clients harness their creativity. This ability enables clients to explore and express new and different ways of thinking, doing, feeling and being. According to psychologist Robert Epstein and his colleagues, there are four core competencies of creative expression:

- *Capturing* our new ideas.
- *Surrounding* ourselves with interesting people and things.
- *Challenging* ourselves by tackling tough problems.
- *Broadening* our knowledge.[37]

One way in which coaches help clients to tap into their creative selves is by ensuring that they stay focused on their goals and that they capture and apply their insights. Coaches also challenge clients to confront their conflicts directly and expand their awareness. They facilitate this process through effective questions that encourage clients to examine themselves, their situation and the other person from different perspectives.

Changing the way we look at a problem—for example, by taking another person's perspective—can induce psychological distance, and this distance in turn can lead to creative ways of addressing the problem.[38] Helping clients gain distance from their conflicts is an important component of conflict management coaching, and readers will soon see how this occurs in the CINERGY™ model.

Positive Reappraisal

> Positive reappraisal facilitates a change in perspective.

Positive reappraisal is an active way of coping with stressful events and is also a strategy for regulating emotions. It has been defined as "a form of meaning-based coping," an "adaptive process by which stressful events are reconstrued as benign, valuable or beneficial."[39] Reappraisal, also known as recontextualizing or reframing, involves re-examination of a situation to discover alternative and less threatening interpretations.

Kevin Ochsner, a psychologist who studies the neuroscience of reappraisal, states that "our emotional responses ultimately flow out of our appraisals of the world and if we can shift those appraisals, we shift our emotional responses."[40] He adds that "the one thing you can always do is control your interpretation of the meaning of the situation."[41] James Gross, a leading expert on emotion regulation, refers also to the fact that among our range of choices is a strategy to make cognitive changes.[42]

Reappraisal, however, takes energy. We must first inhibit our current way of thinking and then generate alternatives that we can hold for a sufficient time to be able to decide which interpretation makes more sense. Besides the required time, effort and focus, reappraisal takes practice.[43]

Acknowledging these realities, coaching offers clients a structured, supported opportunity to concentrate their energies over a protracted period. Over this time, conflict management coaches, help clients reflect on alternative ways of perceiving and experiencing their conflicts, themselves and the other person.

These and other studies in neuroscience contribute to coaches' and clients' understanding of what helps people to gain insights, think reflectively, make decisions and move ahead in new and different ways.

SUMMARY

- Clients come to conflict management coaching with the objective of changing some aspect of their conflict behavior; or, they may want to manage or resolve a dispute with another person. The situation may be in the past, the present or the anticipated future.

- The principles that support the CINERGY™ model of conflict management coaching derive from the three foundational pillars of coaching, mediation and neuroscience.

- Although some practices and principles of mediation are similar to those of the CINERGY™ model of conflict management coaching, mediation and coaching are different processes. The outcomes that individual clients desire from coaching are usually different from what two parties want and expect when participating in mediation.

- The concepts that informed the development of the CINERGY™ conflict management coaching model have their roots in proven principles and practices. They resonate for coaches, mediators, ombudsmen, HR professionals, lawyers, psychologists, leaders, union representatives and others who aim to help people optimize their potential for successfully finding their way through conflict in their personal and professional lives.

Notes

1. Linda J. Page, "Neurosocial Dynamics: Toward a Unique and Cohesive Discipline for Organizational Coaching," *International Journal of Coaching in Organizations* 1 (2009): 104.

2. http://www.coachfederation.org/about-icf/ethics-&-regulation/icf-code-of-ethics.

3. http://www.facebook.com/group.php?gid=22017845353.

4. http://www.certifiedcoach.org/mission/mission.html.

5. http://www.associationforcoaching.com/about/about03.htm.

6. http://www.coachfederation.org/find-a-coach/what-is-coaching.

7. Roger Fisher and William L. Ury, *Getting to Yes: Negotiating Agreement Without Giving In* (New York: Penguin Books, 1981, revised 1991).

8. Robert A. Baruch Bush and Joseph P. Folger, *The Promise of Mediation: Responding to Conflict Through Empowerment and Recognition* (San Francisco: Jossey-Bass, 1994) and Robert A. Baruch Bush and Joseph P. Folger, *The Promise of Mediation: The Transformative Approach to Conflict* (San Francisco: Jossey-Bass, 2005).

9. *Ibid.*, 2.

10. John Winslade and Gerald Monk, *Narrative Mediation: A New Approach to Conflict Resolution* (San Francisco: Jossey-Bass, 2000).

11. Kenneth R. Melchin and Cheryl A. Picard, *Transforming Conflict Through Insight* (Toronto: University of Toronto Press, 2008).

12. *Ibid.*, 79.

13. *Ibid.*, 127.

14. Fredrike Bannink, *Handbook of Solution-Focused Conflict Management* (Cambridge, MA: Hegrefe Publishing, 2010), 20.

15. Daniel J. Siegel, *The Mindful Brain: Reflection and Attunement in the Cultivation of Well-Being* (New York: W.W. Norton, 2007) and Daniel J. Siegel, *Mindsight: The New Science of Personal Transformation* (New York: Bantam Books, 2010).

16. This field is also referred to as social-cognitive-affective neuroscience, and much of the current research is reported in the journal *Social Cognitive and Affective Neuroscience*.

17. David Rock, based on an interview with Jeffrey M. Schwartz, MD, "A Brain-Based Approach to Coaching," *International Journal of Coaching in Organizations* 4 (2006) (2): 36.

18. *Ibid.*

19. David Rock, *Your Brain at Work: Strategies for Overcoming Distraction, Regaining Focus, and Working Smarter All Day Long* (New York: HarperCollins, 2009), 232.

20. David Rock and Linda J. Page, *Coaching with the Brain in Mind: Foundations for Practice* (Hoboken, NJ: John Wiley & Sons, 2009), 185.

21. David Rock, *Your Brain at Work: Strategies for Overcoming Distraction, Regaining Focus, and Working Smarter All Day Long* (New York: HarperCollins, 2009), 232, referring to work by James J. Barrell re: approach versus avoidance, such as Donald D. Price and James J. Barrell, "Some General Laws of Human Emotion: Interrelationships Between Intensities of Desire, Expectations, and Emotional Feeling," *Journal of Personality* 52 (2006) (4): 389–409.

22. *Ibid.*, 232.

23. Jonah Lehrer, "The Eureka Hunt," citing Earl Miller, *The New Yorker* (July 28, 2008), 45.

24. David Rock and Jeffrey Schwartz, "The Neuroscience of Leadership" *Strategy and Business*, 43 (May 30, 2006): 8.

25. Jonah Lehrer, "The Eureka Hunt" *The New Yorker* (July 28, 2008), 40. Some other related references: Jonah Lehrer, *How We Decide* (New York: Houghton Mifflin Harcourt, 2009); A. Bechara, H. Damasio and A. Damasio, "Emotions, Decision Making and the Orbitofrontal Cortex," *Cerebral Cortex* 10 (2000) (3): 295–307.

26. Jonah Lehrer, "The Eureka Hunt" *The New Yorker* (July 28, 2008), 41–43.

27. *Ibid.*, 43.

28. See, e.g., Peter J.D. Carnevale and Alice M. Isen, "The Influence of Positive Affect and Visual Access on the Discovery of Integrative Solutions in Bilateral Negotiation," *Organizational Behavior and Human Decision Processes* 37 (1986) (1): 7–8; Roger Fisher and Daniel L. Shapiro, *Beyond Reason: Using Emotions as You Negotiate* (New York: Penguin, 2005); Barbara L. Fredrickson, "The Role of Positive Emotions in Positive Psychology: The Broaden-and-Build Theory of Positive Emotions," *American Psychologist* 56 (2001): 218–26; Daniel Goleman, *Emotional Intelligence* (New York: Bantam Books, 1995); and Michael Lewis and Jeannette M. Haviland-Jones, *Handbook of Emotions*, 2nd ed. (New York: The Guilford Press, 2000), chapter 27: "Positive Affect and Decision Making," by Alice M. Isen, 417–35.

29. Y.Y. Tang and M.I. Posner, "The Neuroscience of Mindfulness," *NeuroLeadership Journal* 1 (2008): 33.

30. Craig Hassed, "Mindfulness, Wellbeing and Performance," *Neuro-Leadership Journal* 1 (2008): 58, with reference to P. Grossman et al., *Journal of Psychosomatic Research* 57 (2004): 35–43.

31. Jon Kabat-Zim, *Wherever You Go There You Are: Mindfulness Meditation in Everyday Life* (New York: Hyperion, 1994).

32. Douglas K. Silsbee, *The Mindful Coach: Seven Roles for Helping People Grow* (Marshall, NC: Ivy River Press, 2004), 27.

33. Shelley H. Carson and Ellen J. Langer, "Mindfulness and Self-Acceptance," *Journal of Rational-Emotive & Cognitive-Behavior Therapy* 24 (2006) (1): 29–43.

34. Marsha Lucas, "Mindful Meditation + Neuroscience = Healthier Relationships," *Psychology Today* (October 29, 2009), http://www.psychologytoday.com/blog/rewire-your-brain-love/200910/mindfulness-meditation-neuroscience-healthier-relationships.

35. Daniel J. Siegel, *The Mindful Brain: Reflection and Attunement in the Cultivation of Well Being* (New York: W.W. Norton, 2007), 9.

36. *Ibid.*, xiv.

37. Robert Epstein, Steven M. Schmidt and Regina Warfel, "Measuring and Training Creativity Competencies: Validation of a New Test," *Creativity Research Journal* 20 (2008) (1): 7–12.

38. L. Jia, E.R. Hirt and S.C. Karpen, "Lessons from a Faraway Land: The Effect of Spatial Distance on Creative Cognition," *Journal of Experimental Psychology* 45 (2009) (5): 1127–31. Cited in Al Ringleb and David Rock, "NeuroLeadership in 2009," *NeuroLeadership Journal* 2 (2009): 2.

39. Eric Garland, Susan Gaylord and Jongbae Park, "The Role of Mindfulness in Positive Reappraisal," *Explore* 5 (2009) (1): 37.

40. *Ibid.*, 127.

41. David Rock, *Your Brain at Work: Strategies for Overcoming Distraction, Regaining Focus, and Working Smarter All Day Long* (New York: HarperCollins, 2009), 126.

42. James J. Gross and Oliver P. John, "Individual Differences in Two Emotion Regulation Processes: Implications for Affect Relationships and Well-Being," *Journal of Personality and Social Psychology* 85 (2003) (2): 348–62. Cited in David Rock, *Your Brain at Work: Strategies for Overcoming Distraction, Regaining Focus, and Working Smarter All Day Long* (New York: HarperCollins, 2009), 111. See also Kevin N. Oschner and James J. Gross, "The Cognitive Control of Emotion," *Trends in Cognitive Sciences* 9 (2005) (5): 242–49.

43. *Ibid.*

CHAPTER 2

Conflict Management: There Is No Rule Book

Interpersonal conflict is a pervasive, inevitable and normal part of our lives. Academics and practitioners have contributed substantial research and literature to help us understand the causes of interpersonal conflict and its impact on us, those around us and the organizations and systems within which we live, work and play. Training, books, articles and a range of interventions provide us with ways to cope, to interact and to communicate. Despite this assistance, however, many of us do not grasp the dynamic of conflict or our role within it. This chapter examines various elements of interpersonal conflict from the point of view of how it evolves.

Defining Conflict

Interpersonal conflict has been defined as:

> Any situation in which interdependent people have apparently incompatible interests, goals, principles or feelings.[1]

> A condition between two interdependent people in which one or both feel angry at the other and perceive the other as being at fault.[2]

> ... a perceived divergence of interest, or a belief that the parties' current aspirations cannot be achieved simultaneously.[3]

> ... simply the sound made by cracks in a system; regardless of whether the system is personal, relational, familial, organizational, social, economic or political.[4]

Considering these and the many other definitions, the typical main components of conflict include the following:

- At least one person perceives that there is something amiss with another person or persons.
- At least one person experiences negative emotions that prevail indefinitely about a specific interaction with another person or persons.
- Incompatibilities exist about how one person views another's perspectives, actions, words or ways of communicating.

Developing Our Conflict Habits

Those who dread conflict equate it with combat and confrontation and do whatever it takes to contend with it or make it go away. One reason many people avoid interpersonal conflicts and disputes is the anticipated emotional impact that is usually part of such interactions. Our individual histories predispose us to fear our own adverse reactions or those of others, the possibility of irreconcilable outcomes, harsh verbal exchanges, loss of control, high emotions and other unpredictabilities. Such fears and others perpetuate uncertainties about how to manage conflictual situations and tend to preclude our ability to remain clear-headed when there is friction.

Though we are often able to articulate which of our habits are not helpful at these times, they seem to be an automatic part of our defense and coping mechanisms. Even if we forget what a disagreement was about in the first place, as sometimes occurs, unresolved feelings and thoughts often resurface the next time we are in conflict. Unwittingly, we entrench them with each encounter.

These reactions all contribute to the development of habitual ways of managing conflict. Without making a concentrated effort to improve our conflict management skills, we repeat and rely on our default habits for managing interpersonal differences and the strife that accompanies them. These factors, among others, contribute to lack of confidence, anxiety, aversion to discord and counterproductive ways of managing ourselves and other people. It is not surprising, then, that many people do not view conflict as an opportunity to share opinions, create mutually satisfying outcomes or strengthen relationships.

Not everyone avoids conflict or is inept at managing it, of course. Many people have learned effective habits and know whether, when and how to address issues and interpersonal discord. Others enjoy initiating conflict in positive ways, such as to inspire healthy debate. Still others do so with the opposite intention. Conflict management coaches typically meet clients whose habits do not serve them well, and so they seek or are referred for assistance.

The thing is, there is no conflict rule book. Throughout childhood we learn from our parents, guardians, siblings, teachers and friends about ways to be in conflict. These same influences often prevail into adulthood. Bosses, colleagues, peers and others may support our learned habits and, directly or indirectly, teach us more and different ways of managing ourselves and others when in conflict. For many of us, religious, cultural and ethnic backgrounds also influence our perspectives about conflict. Based on these spheres of influence, coupled with our observations, trial and error and so on, we learn what to do, what not to do, what works some of the time in some situations but not in others. Essentially, we develop different ways of reacting to or engaging in disputes, and these ways comprise our individual rule books on conflict.

Our books are fraught with "shoulds," which are both the spoken and unspoken rules that we have scripted over time at conscious, subconscious and unconscious levels. "Shoulds" are mostly based on our own histories and ongoing experiences that we determine as acceptable within the norms of those with whom we live, work and play. There are usually similarities in the "shoulds" shared among family members, chosen friends and the various other people with whom we regularly connect in our personal and professional lives. "Shoulds" are replete with judgment and notions of rightness and wrongness, good and bad. We often express them—with guilt-provoking overtones and implications—to those who do not comply with our "shoulds," or who upset the status quo by deeds, words or behaviors that we deem unacceptable. At these times, we judge them according to our individual frame of reference about what constitutes proper behavior.

What confuses and adds to the tension is that our rules sometimes change just like the numerous people, circumstances and types of interpersonal conflict we encounter. For example, our perception of what is acceptable may depend on the person who says or does something we consider inappropriate, the context, the consequences, our mood, the other person's approach or attitude and other variables. We all have our own list of "shoulds" that we subscribe to, such as, "Leaders should do whatever they can to make sure there is no conflict in the workplace," "people should keep their opinions to themselves if they're going to upset others" and "no one should let others know what they are really feeling." Sometimes, these "shoulds" are attributed to the ubiquitous "they," who seem to know what is morally and socially correct, such as: "They say that you should not question your boss's decisions," or "They say you should never go to bed angry." Our individual rule books comprise these and many other "shoulds," and have the potential for creating conflict with those who do not share our rules and sensibilities about particular actions, behaviors, attitudes and ways of interacting.

In our respective workplaces, "shoulds" about how staff conduct themselves form part of the organizational culture and are considered normative ways of interacting and treating co-workers, those who report to us, bosses, customers and so on. Organizations' concepts of acceptable behaviors may be written in codes of conduct and sometimes in mission statements. Such documents are examples of workplace rule books that reflect the particular expectations inherent in a corporate culture. They are one of the systemic methods for addressing employee relations, including interpersonal conflict.

However, documents of this nature are often subject to interpretation and are not always clearly understood by all employees. Consider a provision such as, "Staff shall communicate respectfully with one another at all times." The word "respectfully" means different things to different people even within the same workplace. As with norms of communication, levels of acceptability and tolerance vary among employees from workplace to workplace. For instance, the customs surrounding staff interactions in hospitals differ from those found in the entertainment industry, or among construction workers on a construction site or teachers in schools. By the same token, the members of subcultures within a workplace usually interact in different ways from other employees in the same organization. As an example, staff members of a finance department communicate differently from the sales staff within the same workplace.

The diversity of workforces, gender and age differences, languages and dialects, and more generally, the disparate mores about managing conflict add further layers to the complexities in establishing and articulating comprehensible and inclusive standards of conduct and communication. This is the case whether or not these standards are documented. Because the rules or "shoulds" differ in the various settings in which we live, work and play, we tend to rely on our individual, time-worn habits. That is, we follow the scripts from our own rule books about how to manage conflict and at some level of consciousness, proceed to test how they fit within our workplaces and relationships.

Based on what we learn in our various interactions, we assimilate, accommodate and adapt as best we can. Most of us commonly find ourselves having to adjust to a range of circumstances and the people that upset us. For all intents and purposes, then, we may change our rules and even some of our seemingly embedded habits at these times.

The CINERGY™ model helps clients identify and re-script the rules that do not work for them. This form of coaching operates on the basis that we have the capacity to change conflict habits and, with intention and practice, can choose and implement different approaches, behaviors and responses.

Before moving on, you may wish to stop here and consider your personal rule book on managing conflict. So, here's the question:

ALL ABOUT YOU

What are some of the "rules" about conflict that you grew up with and that continue to influence how you manage conflict today?

Analyzing Conflicts and Disputes

Undeniably, there are many great models of conflict analysis.[5] In developing the CINERGY™ model of conflict management coaching, however, I chose to engage members of a study group, described in the Introduction, in a process by which they would work individually and together to analyze how their disputes evolved. At the time, I was not yet aware of whether or how this analysis would fit within the coaching process. It occurred to me as a necessary first step in discovering how people's perceptions of their conflicts and disputes may have an impact on building a coaching framework that includes helping them gain different perspectives on themselves, their situations and the other person. The following discussion describes what I learned from the members of the group about the evolution of their conflicts and disputes.

As each group member related three of his or her interpersonal conflicts or disputes, I took copious notes. On close study I found, among other things, that the way the members described their conflict situations followed a sequence that was remarkably similar. Here is a typical scenario, which will next be broken down into the elements that reflect the trajectory that was common among the group's members.

Harold has been getting on my nerves for months now. He has this habit of always having to be right and making everyone else wrong. I have always hated when people do that! It's as though no one else could possibly have a brain in their head. I'm not stupid. All that sanctimony really annoys me. I have lost all patience with this guy. At first I used to think that Harold is just insecure. You know, like the poor guy has to prove something. As time went on and I became more and more annoyed, I figured he is an arrogant know-it-all who doesn't care about anyone but himself. I think he actually enjoys every opportunity to put people down.

The other day the show-off went too far. He interrupted me in a meeting and pontificated on the wrongness of my idea and the rightness of his. I blew up. I couldn't take it any longer and in front of the work team I said, "I'm sick and tired of your righteous attitude, Harold. Others of us have ideas, and yours are not the only ones." The room was silent for what seemed like a very long time. At that point, our Team Leader, Laura, said, "Who else has some thoughts about how to sell this concept?" Some people thought she was being sarcastic in a funny way to lighten the mood, and

> a few people laughed. Mostly, though, everyone looked down and no one responded. There was more silence, and Laura ended the meeting shortly after. Now a bunch of my co-workers are congratulating me. Others are telling me I ought to have chosen another time to blast Harold.

Now, let's break down this scenario into what turned out to be a notably common conflict pathway:

> Harold has been getting on my nerves for months now. He has this habit of always having to be right and making everyone else wrong. I have always hated when people do that!

As members of the study group shared their conflictual interactions, they typically pointed to specific actions or words that a person did or did not do, or said or did not say, that provoked them. As you read in this scenario, the speaker explains that Harold always has to be right and make others wrong, and identifies this as the irritating behavior. In this case, as in many others, the speaker refers to the frequency of the action—"for months now." In a significant number of cases, members also talked about a history of the specific provocation with the same person or more generally with others, such as, "I have always hated when people do that!"

> It's as though no one else could possibly have a brain in their head. I'm not stupid.

After identifying the specific words or actions (or lack of either or both) that precipitated a response in them, study group members conveyed that the other person had challenged one or more values, needs or aspects of their identity. Though those words were not actually used, it was evident that in all cases there was a direct link between the action or words of the other person and the perception that something important to them was being undermined. For example, in this case, the value being undermined has to do with the speaker's intelligence

("I'm not stupid" and "It's as though no one else could possibly have a brain in their head").

All that sanctimony really annoys me. I have lost all patience with this guy.

At this juncture in relating their conflicts, if not before, members described the impact on them when they were triggered in the way they previously described. When they expressed the impact, it was not always in emotional terms, though many talked about their related feelings. Here, for instance, the speaker refers to annoyance and loss of patience. In the study group, some members referred to a physical impact, such as "my stomach turns every time she does that," or a range of other internal responses that reflected the effect on them of the other person's actions or words.

At first I used to think that Harold is insecure. You know, like the poor guy has to prove something. As time went on and I became more and more annoyed, I figured he is an arrogant know-it-all who doesn't care about anyone but himself. I think he actually enjoys every opportunity to put people down.

Study group members then went on to attribute reasons for the other person's provoking behavior. Some people started by giving the other person the benefit of the doubt, as in this case when the speaker says he "used to think that Harold is insecure ... like the poor guy has to prove something." The degree of negativity and intensity, and the nature of the attributions, depended on such variables as who the other person was, how egregious the act or words of provocation were perceived to be and so on. It was also evident that the more deeply the members held the value, need or aspect of their identity that they consciously or unconsciously perceived was being under-mined, the more negative their interpretations were about the other person's underlying motive or intent. In many cases, this state of being in conflict had been going on for a long time, and the reasons identi-fied for the provocation had become progressively more blameful with repetition and frequency. In this scenario, the speaker's attribution evolves to a point that he decides Harold is "an arrogant know-it-all who doesn't care about anyone but himself" and "enjoys every opportunity to put people down."

> **The other day the show-off went too far. He interrupted me in a meeting and pontificated on the wrongness of my idea and the rightness of his.**

In some but not all cases, the study group members experienced that things escalated to a point that crossed a line for them. Language in this regard included phrases such as the other person "went too far," as in this example. Expressions indicating that the other person had pushed a limit of tolerance also included, "It was one time too many," "she pushed the envelope," "that was the straw that broke the camel's back" and "I just couldn't take it any longer." Although the statements often suggested the person could no longer hold in his or her reactions, not all group members necessarily externalized their conflicts by letting the other person know he or she had crossed a boundary. At this point, study group members describing this dynamic were either at a crossroads about whether to say or do anything, or they went on to describe what they said or did in response to the increasingly irritating dynamic.

> **I blew up. I couldn't take it any longer and in front of the work team I said, "I'm sick and tired of your righteous attitude, Harold. Others of us have ideas, and yours are not the only ones."**

As in this statement, if members of the study group said they could no longer contain their feelings or views, they talked about how they outwardly expressed their reactions to the other person. For instance, they may have directly said whatever it was that crossed the line for them. Or, they may have blurted out previous incidents, behaviors and emotions that had built up. In this example, the speaker "blew up" at Harold and let him know what upset him. Study group members described reactions such as "storming out of the room," "stopping any contact," "telling her off," and other ways that people express that someone has pushed them beyond their endurance.

> **The room was silent for what seemed like a very long time. At that point, our Team Leader, Laura, said, "Who else has some thoughts about how to sell this concept?" Some people thought she was being sarcastic in a funny way to lighten the mood, and a few people laughed. Mostly, though, everyone looked down and no one responded. There was more silence, and Laura ended the meeting shortly after. Now a bunch of my co-workers are congratulating me. Others are telling me I ought to have chosen another time to blast Harold.**

Once the conflict was externalized, the study group members described their reactions and the consequences of the event itself on themselves, the other person or both. In many cases, the consequences included the involvement of co-workers, managers or family members.

The (Not So) Merry-Go-Round of Conflict

After observing the above sequence with the study group members and the additional 40 people with whom I tested it and the CINERGY™ model, the initial group and I then developed a schematic to reflect the map of their conflict journeys based on the sequence of thinking and feeling as outlined here. We called the construct that depicted this pathway the (Not So) Merry-Go-Round of Conflict, and it ultimately became a coaching tool for helping clients analyze their conflicts and disputes and gain different perspectives on themselves, their situation and the other person. How it works in practice will be described later in this book. For now, an elaboration of the elements will provide a broader understanding and framework for this particular analysis of conflict.

Before proceeding, however, I want to acknowledge an observation made by Bernard Mayer: "A framework for understanding conflict is an organizing lens that brings conflict into better focus. There are many different lenses we can use to look at conflict, and each of us will find some more amenable to our own way of thinking than others."[6] The following analysis of the conflict dynamic embraces this premise and reflects the lens that I came to appreciate as one way for people to develop self-awareness and reappraise their conflicts and disputes.

Figure 2.1 shows the (Not So) Merry-Go-Round of Conflict framework, which integrates the cognitive, emotional, behavioral and relational dimensions of the human condition in conflict. These were all evident in the stories that the study group members shared. We chose the symbol of the merry-go-round because group members often referred to a circular motion to explain their conflict experience such as, "I went round and round," or "it was like being on a non-stop ferris wheel with him." Several actually used the term "merry-go-round" as a metaphor for how they responded to conflict.

For the purpose of this discussion, here is the operational definition of conflict that evolved from the study group's experiences:

> **Conflict occurs when we perceive that one or more of our values, needs and/or aspects of our identity are being challenged, threatened or undermined by another person.**

To experience the following analytical framework, you may want to focus on a personal or work-related dispute you have had or are currently having to track your own conflict journey, according to elements of Figure 2.1.

FIGURE 2.1   The (Not So) Merry-Go-Round of Conflict

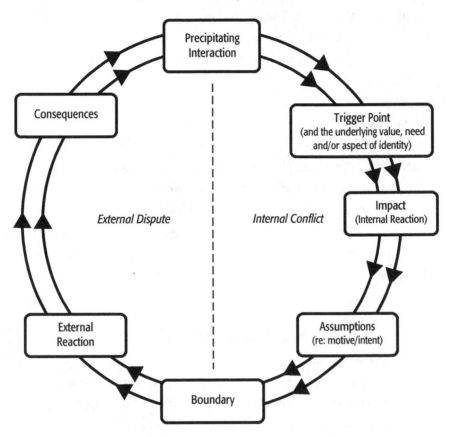

Precipitating Interaction

Precipitating interaction refers to one or more incidents in which we begin to experience discordant thoughts and emotional or other responses about the other person.

The right half of Figure 2.1 encompasses "internal conflict." This includes the inner dialogue and feelings that arise once we are provoked by another person and we begin the journey along our conflict pathway.

The precipitating interaction, located at the top of the diagram, refers to an incident or a series of incidents in which negative or unproductive dynamics with another person start to happen. The internal conversation at these times is usually about initial thoughts and feelings of discomfort, irritation, concerns, apprehensions and other such experiences of provocation. We may sense unease without being able to put our finger on what is going on. Sometimes we are able to let go of our initial response; sometimes we are not. When we express our perspective to others or we mull it over in our heads, our impression of the other person, our own viewpoint and the related emotions begin to take hold and become increasingly entrenched. If we tell friends or family about the other person's actions or words, we may embellish, distort or exaggerate what occurred in order to gain sympathy or support, to make our viewpoint more credible, to defend and justify our response, to take the blame away from ourselves and so on. Our perceptions, however, are our personal reality, and there is no right or wrong about how we experience our conflicts and disputes.

ALL ABOUT YOU

What was the precipitating interaction in the scenario you have in mind? That is, in general terms, what would you say initiated the discord for you?

Trigger Point

The **trigger point** is the specific action or words that the other person does or says, or omits to do or say, that creates negative emotions in us.

Whenever we find ourselves internally responding adversely to a situation, whether it escalates into an outright disagreement or not, there is at least one specific trigger point—the other person's words or actions that specifically irritate us (note the arrow moving downward on the right side of Figure 2.1). It may even be something the other person does not say or do. A trigger point, also called a "hot button" or "flashpoint," may also be an approach, attitude, tone of voice or facial expression that evokes negative emotion in us. The particular trigger in an interaction is an important element of the merry-go-round ride. Focusing on the particular action or words helps to begin the process of unpacking the conflict dynamic. Identifying that point of provocation when we begin the cycle of conflict sometimes requires considerable thought.

> **ALL ABOUT YOU**
>
> *Trigger Point*
>
> In the situation that you chose, what did the other person specifically say or do, or not say or do, when you first noticed there was a negative impact on you?

Values, Needs and Aspects of Identity

Values, needs and aspects of our identity are the fundamental parts of us that we perceive are being challenged, threatened or undermined by the other person's provoking action or words.

In keeping with our definition of conflict, this framework operates on the basis that when people do or say something that pushes a "hot button" for us, there is an underlying sense that something fundamental is being challenged, threatened or undermined. The significance of these elements is discussed here.

Values

Values are our core beliefs and the principles we live by. They reflect the internal maps that guide us in our words and actions. Values are essential to our way of being in the world and of viewing ourselves and others. They represent what we consider right and wrong and form a foundational part of our rule books. Values include the choices we make in our relationships, our vocations and avocations, our friends and even our day-to-day selections about what we wear, the books we read, the movies we prefer and so on. They also account for our motivations, actions and reactions when we are in conflict. Just as our ways of managing conflict have their genesis in a variety of combined and complex sources, the same influences have a major impact on the values we develop. Differences in and lack of acknowledgment of one another's values are often at the root of interpersonal conflict. Identifying the values that we perceive to be undermined when we are provoked is an integral step toward understanding our responses.

Whether or not someone intends to offend us, the intensity of our response when we sense a threat to one or more of our values demonstrates just how important that value is. Other variables, however, may mitigate the intensity of our response. For instance, honesty may be a value you uphold. If someone lies to you, that event may lead to a conflict with that person. Your reaction may depend, though, on who the person is, the issue in question, the attributed intent and so on. This means you may not always react as strongly, and may be more forgiving or understanding in situations with some people who are dishonest with you.

While values reflect our fundamental beliefs, there may be times when we do not act in alignment with them. Let's consider again that honesty is a core value for you. Yet, you may on occasion tell a fib, fabricate a story or essentially lie by purposely omitting some piece of information. If you do any of these you may excuse yourself by saying, "I was afraid of hurting her feelings," or "I didn't have the heart to tell him what really happened." That is, we sometimes rationalize our own actions and make excuses for ourselves that we do not accord to others who provoke us. Moreover, when we act in ways that belie our own values, we experience inner conflict. As a result, we may conduct ourselves in ways that are dissonant—that do not align with our intent— and this dissonance leads to external conflict.

All these layers relating to values are sorted out in conflict management coaching if clients identify that one or more values were undermined for them by the other person's actions or words. Asking clients to define the value that they perceive to be under threat ensures clarity of meaning and sentiment. Consider the value "respect" as an example. When a client is provoked in a conflict and states it was because the other person was disrespectful, it is meaningful for him or her to explore what that signifies in more detail. For instance, the perceived provocation may entail lack of respect for position and authority, for educational achievement, for opinions, for religious beliefs and so on.

Identification of the specific value or values under threat is more powerful when clients identify these for themselves, as the following scenario demonstrates.

Wayne and Michael joined the finance department of the local hospital around the same time about six months ago. They became friends during their accountancy studies, and this was their first job since graduation. What Wayne knew about Michael from their college days was that he tended to be unreliable, and they had had many disputes about this. It wasn't long after they were employed before Wayne saw the same behavior in the workplace. One day Michael was late completing his part of a job, and this meant Wayne was held up. Wayne turned to Michael and, in a raised and angry voice, said he couldn't count on him, that he was irresponsible and that he wasn't going to make excuses for him any longer. Michael walked away, and the two men haven't spoken for days.

Wayne didn't want to go to the manager, so he decided instead to consult with a coach to figure out what to do. Reliability is a meaningful value for Wayne, and he spoke to the coach about the importance he placed on keeping deadlines and being able to count on colleagues. When the coach asked whether he felt anything else was undermined for him through Michael's actions, Wayne thought for a while and then replied that he felt Michael did not respect him as a friend. This was something Wayne had not wanted to consider before, although it had crossed his mind years before in college. He told the coach he thought it was a "silly thing for a grown man to worry about." However, Wayne acknowledged that he had hoped Michael's lack of reliability would not extend to their workplace interactions. Recognizing that it now had and was adversely affecting their relationship, Wayne decided to initiate a serious talk with Michael. He requested further coaching on how to engage Michael in that discussion in such a way that Michael would recognize the gravity of his actions, both personally and professionally.

Needs

Given the second component of the operational definition of conflict, we may perceive that something the other person says or does threatens one or more of our needs. Or, we may perceive that both a value and a need, or a combination of the two, are being undermined. This aspect of the definition of conflict harkens back, in part, to Abraham Maslow's work on human beings' hierarchy of physiological and psychological needs. Our specific hierarchy of workplace and personal needs, however, varies for each of us, and clarifying these with clients is part of conflict management coaching.

Interpersonal conflicts that occur as a result of unmet needs are pervasive and consume much individual and organizational money, time and energy. Some of employees' needs are the obligation of the organization to fulfill. Policies, procedures, rules and regulations, for example, address a range of needs that have been legally and otherwise determined to be requirements for productive, healthy and safe workplaces, for remunerating staff, for vacation periods, for career advancement and so on. Workplace needs may also reflect the extent of a jurisdiction's civil and human rights laws. In unionized workplaces, many provisions of collective agreements represent the components of needs determined as prerequisites for its employees.

Even when an organization has specific policies, procedures and other structures designed to meet its staff members' workplace needs, conflict arises when such policies do not meet these needs to employees' satisfaction.

One need that is often minimized or overlooked by organizations is the social need for co-workers to connect with one another and with their leaders. Yet, many workplaces do not consider relationship issues as their responsibility, nor do they understand the importance of providing the means for addressing interpersonal workplace conflict to help staff reconcile their differences.

In reality, for many people, the requirement to earn an income takes precedence over asserting other fundamental needs. In these cases, staff members perceive they do not have the luxury of expressing their needs, fearing repercussions such as losing their job or being relegated to unsatisfying work.

Identifying unmet or challenged needs that underlie the actions and words that provoke us is not typically a straightforward process. As with values, people are not always conscious that conflict is a result of their unmet needs, or that their needs are at odds with someone else's. Further, staff members do not know whether their unmet workplace needs are a result of the organization's or their leaders' or co-workers' lack of willingness or capacity to provide them. Needs that are unmet by a partner or spouse, friends, family members and neighbors also lead to personal conflicts. Whatever the case, identifying needs and their meaning helps clients recognize the factors that exacerbate their responses. The real-life scenario that follows illustrates the importance of clients' clarifying their needs.

Clara started out as a teller in a bank three years ago and worked hard to become the manager of a busy branch. She still lacked a number of skills and was trying to learn what she could through an online course for new managers. Finding it difficult to learn that way, Clara became frustrated and

asked the District Manager whether it was possible to get a mentor instead or perhaps to have meetings with other new branch managers dedicated to this learning. Clara's District Manager told Clara to "just get with the 21st century and use the computer like everyone else."

When Clara met with a coach to discuss what she wanted to do about this situation, she identified that besides the manner in which the District Manager berated her, his out-right denial of her request was a huge trigger for her. Clara went on to describe that she learns best through interaction with others. Even more so, she found the isolation of her position difficult without the collegiality of other managers with whom to discuss work-related matters, including the topics in the online learning program. Ultimately, with coaching, Clara decided she wanted to make a plan to initiate a New Managers group. She discovered, when she contacted a few she had met at a recent meeting, that she was not alone in the need for a personal connection and sense of belonging that online learning did not provide. She also obtained assistance in preparing what she wanted to say to her District Manager about her plan and his reaction to her requests.

Identity

Identity, the third component of the operational definition about what may cause conflict, has a number of subcomponents. "Identity" is a broad term; it relates, in part, to how we view our status or role in our professional or personal lives and may also reflect our values and our needs. How we describe our identity also expresses how we perceive ourselves and want to be perceived in terms of our relative importance to others.

Some aspects of identity are gender, age, birth order, skin color, certain physical traits, generation and ethnicity. Other components of our identity are those we intentionally select. These may include our vocation, place of work or residence, avocations, marital status, relationships, political choices and so on. Positions to which we are elected or appointed—such as manager, CEO, politician—represent another type of status. Different attitudes, personality and character traits, skills and behaviors may contribute to how we define our individual identity too, such as being extroverted, talkative or aggressive.

Most commonly, we consider our identity in the aggregate ("I am a coach, a great parent, an outdoorswoman and an avid reader") and spend considerable time and energy developing various aspects of who we are, who we want to be and how we want to be seen. However, we may not be fully conscious that we do so or why, nor do we necessarily acknowledge our efforts to cultivate our identity.

Conflicts that emerge from perceived threats to how we see ourselves often arise in the workplace and other contexts and can have an enormous impact on us. Exploring and understanding the aspects of our identities that are important to us, then, helps us gain insights about what is likely to provoke us and lead to conflict. As with values and needs, our perspectives on how we describe our identify are subjective and are sometimes challenging to articulate. Similarly, we may not be fully aware that we sense a challenge to an aspect of our identity or status, or which particular aspect, until further examination, as the following real-life scenario demonstrates.

For as long as he could remember, Greg wanted to be a lawyer and worked hard to get on the honor roll at law school. He got a job at a major law firm and became a partner in record time. At a party recently, Greg was standing with a group when someone was telling a joke about the legal profession. Greg thought it was funny and laughed along. One of the people in the group said, "Greg, it's good you can laugh at yourself. I never thought you really looked like a lawyer anyway." Greg was offended by these remarks and reacted strongly, resulting in a dispute between him and the joke-teller about the virtues of the legal profession.

Several weeks earlier, Greg had retained a coach to help him better manage conflict and understand what leads to his often defensive reactions and arguments with others. Using this scenario as one example, he reflected on what really provoked him, and identified that it was not only the remarks about his profession that upset him. His response had more to do with what he perceived as an insult to his appearance. A few months previously, he had retained an image consultant to help with his "boyish" looks. He wanted to look more professional and mature. This was an issue with which Greg had grappled for years and was embarrassed to admit. Once he expressed this to the coach, he gained more awareness about his defensive reactions related to the image he strives to project.

Through coaching, Greg became more adept at reflecting on his reasons for reacting and the emotions he was feeling at the time. He ultimately gained skills to better regulate his emotions and respond to perceived affronts in a way he preferred.

The CINERGY™ model assists individuals to explore the link between their trigger points and the underlying values, needs or aspects of their identity as part of a broader analysis of understanding the conflict dynamic and why they react to certain words and actions. The utility of this approach is evident in the way that such realizations assist clients to begin the process of unbundling their conflict patterns and looking at their situation from a different perspective.

At this time, you might wish to pause and consider the following exercise to determine how the suggested operational definition of conflict applies to you.

ALL ABOUT YOU

When the other person provoked you in the way you described as the trigger point …

Values

Which of your values, if any, would you say were undermined?

Needs

Consider whether you perceived that the other person also (or instead) undermined one or more of your needs. If so, what was it (were they)?

Identity

Reflecting again on that interaction and the trigger point, if you perceived that the other person's actions or words challenged some part of your identity, what aspect(s) was (were) undermined?

Impact

This component of the (Not So) Merry-Go-Round of Conflict is the next element going downward on the right side of Figure 2.1.

Internal reaction (impact) refers to the effect on us when the other person provokes us with specific actions or words (the trigger point).

Inevitably, when we have been offended about something important to us, we experience an emotional effect. We may feel angry, defensive, humiliated, hurt, disappointed, fearful, guilty, betrayed and so on. In any given conflict, identifying and exploring the internal reaction (impact) helps us understand more about our sensibilities as they relate to the specific trigger point. "Internal reaction," as it is described here, also includes the feelings we may have accumulated about the other person based on any history we have with him or her. Historical experiences of being provoked by the same "hot button" with the same person generally tend to taint the impact to a greater extent than a single episode. Repeated provocations also typically serve to entrench our judgments and strengthen our perspective on this person and any specific issues in dispute.

Other impacts may include loss of sleep, stomach turning, fretting that co-workers or the boss are aware of the conflict and may get involved and so on. The stronger we experience the sense of being undermined, and the stronger our attachment to the value, need or aspect of our identity underlying the trigger point, the stronger the impact and the more our rational thinking, judgment and communication skills deteriorate. As our emotions escalate, there are various other repercussions. Self-limiting beliefs may envelop our internal responses with the accompanying self-talk and questioning, such as, "She must think I'm weak," or, "He is laughing at me." Some people may also (or alternatively) engage in blame.

When feelings about the other person deepen, our perspectives often stray farther from reality. We may experience and demonstrate various emotions and other symptoms of distress when we are initially provoked. However, the impact at this juncture is usually an internal reaction, and we have not yet externalized our response to the other person. That is, we are still on the right side of the schematic (Figure 2.1) referred to as "internal conflict."

Conflict management coaching works as an effective, proactive modality that may be initiated as soon as people are triggered and there is an impact that creates internal upset. However, people do not typically seek coaching assistance at this early point along the conflict pathway, when they might be able to short-circuit unnecessary escalation.

ALL ABOUT YOU

Impact

How would you describe the impact on you when you were triggered by the other person in the scenario that you are unbundling?

If you have a history with this person, what feelings have you accumulated about him or her over time?

Interpretations/Assumptions

Interpretations/assumptions regarding motive or intent refer to the act of attributing reasons to the other person for what he or she said or did (or didn't say or do) that provoked us.

Moving downward again on the right side of Figure 2.1, the next element in the conflict sequence is the common inclination to attribute reasons for the other person's conduct.[7] When making assumptions about why people do what they do, we again draw on our habits, rules and other influences from our previous experiences. In the process of considering the reasons for the other person's actions or words, we may initially accord benign motives. However, attributions commonly become distorted, self-serving, self-blaming or fault-finding. Again, the deeper we hold the value, need or aspect of our identity and the stronger the impact of the perceived provocation, the more negatively we infer the other person's intent. The accumulation of such dynamics serves to strengthen and support our positions and emotions. As our reasoning continues to decline and our feelings increase in intensity, there is a tendency to judge the other person's character in increasingly demeaning ways.

ALL ABOUT YOU

Assumptions About the Other Person's Motives or Intent

For what reasons may the other person have said or done (or not said or done) what you identified as your specific trigger point in your situation?

Boundary

Boundary refers to the limit of our tolerance for the other person's actions or words.

The internal conflict we experience in the trajectory of the conflict depicted by the right side of the (Not So) Merry-Go-Round of Conflict (Figure 2.1) may linger indefinitely. We may conceal our thoughts and feelings from the other person and not express that we are upset and why. However, we are still experiencing inner conflict, and these feelings can flare up, progressing along the conflict pathway, in a nanosecond. Or, months or years may go by before something happens that shifts the dynamic from internal to external manifestation in which we engage the other person. Or, things may never escalate, yet suppressed feelings remain.

Boundary—the next element in the conflict sequence—is pictured at the bottom of Figure 2.1. It is the line that is crossed when the other person does or says something to push us beyond the limits of tolerance. When a conflict is internal, people who know and observe us (including the other person) may pick up on our tension and be aware of a discordant dynamic. That tension usually becomes more obvious when a boundary is crossed for us, unless we are able to continue suppressing our emotions. If we do react outwardly, we often do so in counter-productive ways. The externalization of the conflict means the other person becomes aware of the adverse effect that his or her words or actions have had on us. This typically, but not always, engages him or her to react. When the other person reacts and both people are engaged, the situation becomes a dispute. The left side of Figure 2.1 depicts the "external dispute" once things have escalated and are now overt.

Our boundaries vary widely and are, of course, subjective. Some of us may identify our trigger point and boundary in a given situation as being one and the same, such as when we are provoked once too often by a person's specific actions or words. What crosses a boundary and what pushes a trigger point, however, are often different, and they may happen simultaneously or at different times.

For example, let's say you are triggered by your co-worker Bryan. You perceive and identify the trigger point as his act of continually undermining the quality of your marketing ideas. You have traveled along your pathway on the right side of the (Not So) Merry-Go-Round of Conflict (Figure 2.1), experiencing increased annoyance and attributing more and more malevolent motives each time Bryan comments on your ideas in derogatory ways. So far you have not reacted outwardly, although you are seething inwardly. Then one day in front of a client, Bryan questions your efforts on the latest joint project. His act of undermining your work remains the trigger point. Doing so in front of the customer, however, crosses the line for you.

ALL ABOUT YOU

Boundary

If, in your situation, the other person crossed one of your boundaries, what was it that he/she said or did that went too far for you?

External Reaction

External reaction is what we say or do when we respond outwardly to the person who crosses our line of tolerance.

The next element, external reaction, pointing upward from "boundary" on the left side of Figure 2.1, refers to our outward expression or actions when a boundary is crossed. At these times, attributions and reactions that were activated when we begin to experience internal conflict become stronger and take expression in ways that reflect our increased level of irritation, negativity and emotion. They also demonstrate our individual ways of responding when things go too far for us.

The degree to which we externalize our feelings when someone crosses our boundary depends on such factors as how strongly we experience the affront, our individual ways of reacting in conflict, our ability to regulate our emotions, our tendencies to suppress our feelings, what and who crossed the line, the historical relationship, the stakes and so on. We may demonstrate behaviors that have been reinforced by repeated usage whether or not we or others like them. We may also have a history of getting what we want with our ways of reacting and have limited incentive to change them. We may not think it is possible to change, or we may lack opportunities to learn alternative ways of coping.

Possible reactions when our boundaries are crossed:

- Some reactions are impulsive. We feel out of control of our actions or words. We may say something to retaliate or counter the other person's actions or comments. We may swear, cry or yell. We may walk away, or we may say things that we regret immediately or later. Sometimes we may react in non-verbal ways or to the point of physical aggression or even violence.
- Other reactions may be physiological, such as when our face gets red, our heart races, our muscles tense, our hands shake and so on.
- Still other reactions may be intellectual, as when we rationalize our own or the other person's behavior. Intellectualizing when someone crosses our boundary reflects an effort to make logical sense of what is happening at a time when we are least likely able to do so.

At this point in the cycle, whether we are reacting impulsively, physiologically or intellectually, it is common that our body, face and actions demonstrate a range of emotions. Even if we do not outwardly express what we are feeling, it is often apparent to the other person and any observers that there is discord.

The reality for many people is that we are not fully aware, in the moment, of what is happening when we react to the experience of being pushed beyond our level of tolerance. Not only do we usually lack a full picture of what is going on for ourselves; we are also not conscious of what is going on for the other person, including the impact of our reactions on them.

Upon reflection, we likely can identify when and how we respond in ways that keep us riding around on our merry-go-rounds of conflict and which may even serve to start the other person on his or her own merry-go-round ride.

ALL ABOUT YOU

External Reaction

If, in your situation, the other person crossed one of your boundaries and you reacted externally, how did you do so?

Consequences

Consequences are the result and effect when we react to someone's crossing one of our boundaries.

Though one or both people may stay in the right side of the merry-go-round indefinitely, once one person externally reacts and engages the other person, there is usually fallout for both people. The element of conflict that occurs then (progressing upward on the left side of Figure 2.1) is consequences.

Undeniably, inner conflicts have consequences. However, the escalation of a conflict into a dispute produces many more far-reaching effects. For instance, the people in a dispute may act aggressively toward each other, engage others in discussing the issues, ignore each other altogether and so on. The net effect is commonly that the increased tension in the relationship spills over to work productivity, personal lives and co-workers.

Moreover, external reactions further perpetuate the progressive and escalating course of a conflict as each person repeatedly triggers the other with his or her respective external reactions. Under such circumstances, the cycle represented in Figure 2.1 is continuously activated and reactivated, going round and round, leading to increasingly more trigger points being pushed for both, more values, needs and aspects of identity being challenged, more intense impacts, more attributions, more boundaries being crossed and so on.

ALL ABOUT YOU

Consequences

- In your situation, what were the consequences for you when you reacted to your boundary being crossed (if applicable)?
- What were the consequences for the other person?
- What were the consequences for others?

Sharing the Ride on the Merry-Go-Round

People in a dispute may seem to have little in common. However, we all routinely play out habitual conflict patterns that are activated once we are provoked. When we are able to stand back and observe the sequence, the awareness we gain is pivotal for understanding ourselves in conflict.

The important point here is that we get on the merry-go-round ride not only because of someone else's actions or words. We, too, may initiate the conflict cycle in the other person. In either case, the two arrows that surround the (Not So) Merry-Go-Round of Conflict (Figure 2.1) demonstrate the separate but same trajectory for ourselves and for those with whom we are in conflict or dispute.

What in fact propelled further insights for study group members after they first became aware of their own conflict habits and patterns was the act of stepping into the other person's shoes and following his or her pathway using the same elements. This journey into mutuality was based on group members' observations and experience with the other person in their interaction.

Ultimately, conducting this analysis helped study group members gain different perspectives from the ones they initially had. It further assisted them in gaining some objectivity and understanding about the other person's point of view.

ALL ABOUT THE OTHER PERSON

Now, it's time to walk in the other person's shoes in the dispute you are exploring for yourself by following the sequence of all the elements in the (Not So) Merry-Go-Round of Conflict (Figure 2.1).

- What would the other person's perspective be about what started the discord between you?
- What specific thing did you say or do (or not say or do) that seemed to provoke the other person?
- What value, need or aspect of his/her identity might you have challenged when you provoked him/her?
- From what you observed, what was the impact on the other person when you triggered him/her?
- What reasons might he/she have attributed to you for provoking him/her?
- What might have crossed his/her boundary?
- What was/were his/her external reaction(s) at that point?
- What were the personal consequences of his/her reaction(s)?
- What were the consequences for you?
- What were the consequences for others (if applicable)?

Further Grounding for the Elements of Conflict

The trajectory described in Figure 2.1 is grounded in more than the reported experiences of the study group members and clients who subsequently engaged in the CINERGY™ process. Based on a model of emotional generation–regulation that was first proposed by James Gross, Kevin Ochsner's elaboration on Gross's work provides further credibility to the sequence described, once we become provoked in conflict. The bracketed words in italics in the following description of Ochsner's theory are mine. They reflect the connections I have extrapolated from his findings that compare with the elements of conflict in the (Not So) Merry-Go-Round of Conflict that were identified experientially in the development of the CINERGY™ model.

According to Ochsner, the process of generating an emotion starts when a situation stimulates us in some way followed by selected attention on one of the stimuli [what I have called a *trigger point*]. He explains that the next step entails an appraisal of the meaning of that cue within the context of our current goals, wants and needs [*values, needs, identity*]. We may then make excuses for the person or assess the meaning in a way that is offensive, threatening or worrisome for us [*assumptions/interpretations regarding motive or intent*]. Once we make the appraisal, there is an impact on us that may be emotional, behavioral or physiological [*impact*]. Ochsner further notes that emotions are continuously generated by a cyclical process that is taking place and that it is not only stimuli that drive emotion, but also the responses we make [*external reaction*] and the effects of our behaviors [*consequences*].[8]

In the end, the lens that the "merry-go-round" provides for analyzing conflicts and disputes became a way for study group members to reframe their situations and the dynamics between them and the other person. How this process is integrated within the CINERGY™ model will be further discussed in Chapter 4.

Emotions in Conflict

A discussion on conflicts and disputes is incomplete without expanding on the subject of emotions and feelings. Emotion is one of the main dimensions of conflict, and identifying the feelings clients experience about their conflictual events is an important part of their coaching journey.

There are many possible definitions of emotion. One basic one is that emotions are "brief, rapid responses involving physiological, experiential, and behavioral activity that help humans respond to survival-related problems and opportunities."[9] Emotions tell us and others that we care and what we care about, and they may cause or escalate conflicts when we ignore them.[10] According to David Rock, emotions represent "an integration of brain/body mind and social information sources. They serve as 'great summarizers' of our current frame of mind."[11]

Emotions assist coaches in helping clients to explore and understand the basis on which they construct meaning for their experience-associated reactions. A typical cycle of emotions when we are in conflict is as follows:

- We experience unsettling sensations regarding something that matters to us.
- Physical changes may occur.
- Thoughts emerge in relation to the emotions we feel.
- There is a desire to act on the emotion.

Conflict management coaches listen to the words that clients use to refer to their emotions about their conflicts and encourage them to describe these statements. While developing the CINERGY™ model and in coaching, I noted numerous words that clients repeatedly used in response to a question about naming the emotions they experience when they are provoked by the other person's specific acts or words. Appendix III lists many of the common ones. It is also noteworthy that when discussing emotions, people may express fears about their experience of being in conflict. According to Joseph LeDoux, a fore-most researcher on fear:

> Anxiety and fear are closely related. Both are reactions to harmful or potentially harmful situations. Anxiety is usually distinguished from fear by the lack of external stimulus that elicits the reaction—anxiety comes from within us, fear from the outside world.[12]

Appendix IV lists common fears expressed in workplace conflicts and disputes.

Coaches also pay close attention to the fact that emotions extend beyond what we say and feel. Often our body and face are the first identifiers of emotions. Neuroscientist Alfred Damasio states:

> The "main stage" or "theatre" for all emotions is the body because emotions and bodily responses are so closely linked. It is in the body that the first indicators of an emotion are felt and can be recognized. When strong negative emotions are recognized early, they can be dealt with more effectively, and the reasons why they arose can be addressed more quickly. The ability to recognize emotions—especially strong negative emotions—in the body is made easier by understanding their corresponding physical signs.[13]

What Drives Emotions in Conflict?

"Emotional drivers" are the subject of much research. As part of the conflict management process, coaches help clients gain self-awareness in this regard, too.

Various commentators have identified motivators of emotions that generate a fight, flight, or freeze response. Examples of drivers are those from the operational definition of conflict used in the CINERGY™ model—i.e., conflict occurs when we perceive that one or more of our values, needs or an aspect of our identities is challenged, threatened or undermined.

In their book, *Beyond Reason: Using Emotions as You Negotiate*, Roger Fisher and Daniel Shapiro refer to five core concerns requiring effective management to be able to create positive emotions between disputing parties in a mediation or other ADR process. These are:

> *appreciation* (acknowledgment of the value of the thoughts, emotions and actions of the other person and helping the other person appreciate ours), *affiliation* (developing connections with another person by building trust, treating each other respectfully and so on), *autonomy* (respecting the freedom and right of people to make decisions for themselves), *status* (recognizing that the other person and ourselves hold a status that is special and important to each of us) and *role* (acknowledging and supporting our respective roles and that they provide a clear, meaningful purpose).[14] [Emphasis added.]

Within the context of leadership coaching and from a neuroscience perspective, David Rock discusses the SCARF model. This acronym refers to five activators of the limbic part of the brain: threats to *S*tatus (where we stand relative to others in the social order of the workplace and other communities in which we work and live), *C*ertainty (our ability to call on previous experiences to predict and manage new and different situations and the future), *A*utonomy (having control of choices), *R*elatedness (the sense of belonging and being safely and trustingly connected to people around us) and *F*airness (the process and state of interacting in which people act ethically, transparently and otherwise appropriately with one another).[15]

Other commentators view the motivators of emotions in conflict somewhat differently. Bernard Mayer, in his book, *The Dynamics of Conflict Resolution: A Practitioner's Guide*, refers to "identity-based needs" as "community, intimacy and autonomy."[16] Douglas Stone, Bruce Patton and Sheila Heen, in their book *Difficult Conversations: How to Discuss What Matters Most*, speak of the three core identities in the form of questions: "Am I competent?," "Am I a good person?" and "Am I worthy of love?"[17]

It is notable that identity, defined in similar terms as status and role, is common to all these examples of what triggers emotion for people in conflict.

One common source of emotions, according to leading researcher Paul Ekman, is the perception that someone or something will have an impact on our well-being. When this happens, which is often the case for people in conflict, we remain vigilant about possible threats that can instantly trigger emotions in us. Ekman gave the term *auto-appraising* to the applicable brain process that regularly monitors our environment. He states that humans share some common emotions and learn others based on our individual and unique life experiences, adding that when certain themes occur, our emotions arise. As indicated in the experiences of the study group members, these themes may include the actions and words that trigger us, as well as those that cross our boundaries. Importantly, auto-appraisers are not necessarily accurate assessments of threatening situations. We may perceive threats that do not exist and yet, we still react.[18]

Relative to this concept, neuroscientist Evian Gordon says that much of the motivation that drives social behavior is governed by an overarching organizing principle of minimizing threat and maximizing reward. He calls it "the fundamental organizing principle of the brain."[19] The brain likes certainty, and neurons are activated when we experience something new. When we perceive a threat, part of the brain (the amygdala) signals a stress response that includes the release of cortisol, which is part of the sympathetic nervous system's flight-or-fight response. When hormones are released in reaction to potential threats, we seek to determine whether this new experience represents a chance for reward or danger. The effect of such a response includes a reduction in problem-solving, decision-making, motivation and other major brain functions.

Emotional Impact of Conflict: Other Outcomes

Daniel Goleman, in his book *Emotional Intelligence*, refers to the state of inappropriate arousal as "amygdala hijack," which may lead to a range of outcomes, including generalizing. In this response, mental maps are activated that are unrelated, or are only tangentially related, to the situation. Goleman also refers to the ways in which the reasoning, decision-making and problem-solving parts of the prefrontal cortex are compromised because amygdala arousal reduces the flow of energy to this portion of the brain. In addition, there is a tendency to err on the side of pessimism because the output of the amygdala is fear and anxiety, and "ambiguous input ends up feeling like doom."[20]

Besides the findings that ongoing stress inhibits cognitive functioning, including the working memory, it reduces the capacity to process and store information.[21] It has also been found that "higher prefrontal cortex activity is associated with lower limbic activity" and, according to some researchers, "this finding suggests that putting feelings into words may activate a part of the prefrontal cortex that suppresses the area of the brain that produces emotional distress."[22] In this regard, cognitive neuroscientist Matthew Leiberman states that

> [n]aming an emotion calms the amygdala. Talking about it changes the feelings. Trying to suppress it maintains arousal and interferes with prefrontal processing such as seeing the big picture, regulating one's emotions or empathy.[23]

Leiberman and other researchers at the University of California at Los Angeles have further identified that "psychological pain such as insults and rejection show up in the same part of the brain as physical pain."[24]

Clients who are unable to make sense of their conflictual interactions and the accompanying emotions commonly come to coaching with various of the above-mentioned brain functions impaired. When assisting people through their conflicts, coaches remain alert to clients' readiness and ability to proceed before they have expressed and named the emotional repercussions of their conflicts and disputes.

Venting and Suppressing Emotions

Some clients willingly discuss their emotions about their conflicts. Others will resist talking about their feelings because of denial, embarrassment, habits learned about holding back, lack of trust, resistance to what may be perceived as intrusiveness or therapeutic intervention, cultural influences, language challenges such as in finding words to articulate feelings, anxiousness to move forward, fear of losing control or being seen as someone who is weak and so on.

Though it is a fact that suppressing emotions has a deleterious impact on our mental functioning[25] and can cause physical problems for ourselves and those with whom we share our personal and professional lives,[26] it is a way of coping. Clients may take a while to express their emotional experience of conflict, if they do at all. It is important to also acknowledge that emotional repercussions may linger after conflict is ostensibly over. Many of us become better able to see our situations in a new light only after dissolution of the residual effect[27]; the stronger the intensity of the emotion, the longer the recovery time.[28] These variables are further reminders for coaches that it may take time for some clients to express and process the emotional impact of their conflicts and disputes before they are able to make decisions about whether and how to take some action regarding their coaching goals.

While most practitioners agree on the importance of giving people the opportunity to vent, there are reported limitations on venting.[29] Discussing conflict situations for too long may keep clients in a place of stress and negativity. When they are overwhelmed with emotion about their situation and the people who upset them, staying in an emotional place essentially precludes movement forward and the ability to reason and problem-solve.

Recognizing the fine balance between acknowledging a client's emotions and moving forward requires skill. The main considerations include the necessity for coaches to recognize the emotional element of clients' conflicts, and also to be able to help them transition to a place from which they will be able to move ahead. This topic is dealt with in greater detail in Chapter 5.

SUMMARY

- We all develop habitual ways of managing conflict, including how we experience it relationally, cognitively, emotionally and behaviorally. The habits we learn become our individual rule books. Through coaching, we have the ability to change these rule books and re-script our "shoulds."

- Conflict management coaching gives clients the opportunity to reflect on how they respond and react to conflict as part of a process to gain self-awareness and consider new and different ways of engaging with others.

- Interpersonal conflict gives rise to many emotions, including fear of the unknown and uncertainty of the interaction and its outcome. Fear of hurtful words and actions, perceived threats, possible loss of the relationship and shame or guilt over our own behavior are some of the many emotions that fuel our reactions and the ways we cope.

- When we are in dispute with another person, we commonly follow a pathway with sequential steps. By exploring the elements that contribute to the evolution of conflicts and disputes, clients gain insights into themselves and the other person, as well as increased understanding of what precipitates and exacerbates the friction and emotions for both parties.

- Figure 2.1, the (Not So) Merry-Go-Round of Conflict (page 51), presents an exercise in developing mutuality. The schematic describes the elements along the route of conflict that help people analyze interpersonal disputes from their own perspective and from that of the other person.

- Emotions are critical components of conflict. They demonstrate how and why we create meaning about parts of our lives such as the values, needs and aspects of our identity that are important to us. Threats to these components of ourselves are major drivers of emotion, and challenges to one or more of these areas have an impact on our ability to reason, problem-solve and make decisions.

- The degree to which clients are willing to share their emotional reactions to their conflicts varies. Both suppressing emotion and over-venting pose potential challenges in helping clients think out and decide how to move ahead in their conflict management goals.

- Conflict management coaches help clients "think about their thinking" and recognize that they need emotions to be able to reason and make decisions. Knowing when and how to help a client progress from processing emotions through reasoning and analysis is a learned skill that takes practice, strong intuition and a solid connection with clients.

Notes

1. Craig E. Runde and Tim A. Flanagan, *Becoming a Conflict Competent Leader: How You and Your Organization Can Manage Conflict Effectively* (San Francisco: Jossey-Bass, 2007), 22. Initially derived from the definition by Sal Capobianco, Mark Davis and Linda Kraus, *Conflict Dynamics Profile* (St. Petersburg, FL: Eckerd College Leadership Development Institute, 1999).

2. Daniel Dana, *Managing Differences: How to Build Better Relationships at Work and Home* (Prairie Village, KS: MTI Publications, 2005), 224.

3. Jeffrey Rubin, Dean G. Pruitt and Sung Hee Kim, *Social Conflict: Escalation, Stalemate, and Settlement*, 2nd ed. (New York: McGraw-Hill, 1986), 5.

4. Kenneth Cloke, *The Crossroads of Conflict: A Journey into the Heart of Dispute Resolution* (Santa Ana, CA: Janis Publications, 2006), 18.

5. To name a few texts that include conflict analyses: Gary T. Furlong, *The Conflict Resolution Toolbox: Models and Maps for Analyzing,*

Diagnosing, and Resolving Conflict (Toronto: John Wiley & Sons Canada, 2005); Bernard S. Mayer, *The Dynamics of Conflict Resolution: A Practitioner's Guide* (San Francisco: Jossey-Bass, 2000); Kenneth R. Melchin and Cheryl A. Picard, *Transforming Conflict Through Insight* (Toronto: University of Toronto Press, 2008); Christopher W. Moore, *The Mediation Process: Practical Strategies for Resolving Conflict*, 3rd ed. (San Francisco: Jossey-Bass, 2003).

6. Bernard S. Mayer, *The Dynamics of Conflict Resolution: A Practitioner's Guide* (San Francisco: Jossey-Bass, 2000), 4.

7. Much has been written about attribution theory. See, for example, Chris Argyris, *Overcoming Organizational Defenses: Facilitating Organizational Learning* (Englewood Cliffs, NJ: Prentice Hall, 1990); Chris Argyris and Donald A. Schon, *Theory in Practice: Increasing Professional Effectiveness* (San Francisco: Jossey-Bass, 1974); Dennis T. Regan, Ellen Straus and Russell Fazio, "Liking and the Attribution Process," *Journal of Experimental Social Psychology* 10 (1974) (4); Bernard Weiner, "On Sin Versus Sickness: A Theory of Perceived Responsibility and Social Motivation," *American Psychologist* 48 (1993) (9); Daryl Landau, "Attributions in Conflict: Changing the Blame Game," *Canadian Arbitration and Mediation Journal* 19 (2010) (1); Bertram Gawronski, "Theory-Based Bias Correction in Dispositional Inference: The Fundamental Attribution Error Is Dead, Long Live the Correspondence Bias," *European Review of Social Psychology* 15 (2004).

8. Kevin Ochsner, "Staying Cool Under Pressure: Insights from Social Cognitive Neuroscience and Their Implications for Self and Society," (2008), *Neuroleadership Journal* 1 (2008) (1): 32, with reference to James J. Gross, "The Emerging Field of Emotion Regulation: An Integrative Review," *Review of General Psychology* 2 (1998) (3): 271–99; Kevin N. Ochsner and James J. Gross, "The Neural Architecture of Emotion Regulation," Chapter 5 in James J. Gross, ed., *Handbook of Emotion Regulation* (New York: The Guilford Press, 2007); Klaus R. Scherer, Angela Schorr and Tom Johnstone (eds.), *Appraisal Processes in Emotion: Theory, Methods, Research* (New York: Oxford University Press, 2001).

9. D. Keltner and P. Ekman, "Emotion: An Overview," in Alan E. Kazdin, ed., *Encyclopedia of Psychology* (London: Oxford University Press, 2000), 163.

10. According to David Rock and Linda J. Page, *Coaching with the Brain in Mind: Foundations for Practice* (Hoboken, NJ: John Wiley & Sons, 2009), feelings ("subjective experiences of emotions") have been studied more as a sensation by the fields of physiology, anatomy and psychophysiology. We tend to use the words to mean much the same and use them interchangeably, and I do so in this book.

11. David Rock and Linda J. Page, *Coaching with the Brain in Mind: Foundations for Practice* (Hoboken, NJ: John Wiley & Sons, 2009), 342–46.

12. Joseph LeDoux, *The Emotional Brain: The Mysterious Underpinnings of Emotional Life* (New York: Simon and Schuster, 1996), 228.

13. Antonio R. Damasio, *The Feeling of What Happens: Body and Emotion in the Making of Consciousness* (San Diego, CA: Harcourt, 1999), 39.

14. Roger Fisher and Daniel Shapiro, *Beyond Reason: Using Emotions as You Negotiate* (New York: Penguin Group, 2005).

15. David Rock, *Your Brain at Work: Strategies for Overcoming Distraction, Regaining Focus, and Working Smarter All Day Long* (New York: HarperCollins, 2009), 276.

16. Bernard S. Mayer, *The Dynamics of Conflict Resolution: A Practitioner's Guide* (San Francisco: Jossey-Bass, 2000), 17.

17. Douglas Stone, Bruce Patton and Sheila Heen, *Difficult Conversations: How to Discuss What Matters Most* (New York: Penguin Putnam, 1999).

18. From reference in Craig E. Runde and Tim A. Flanagan, *Becoming a Conflict Competent Leader: How You and Your Organization Can Manage Conflict Effectively* (San Francisco: Jossey-Bass, 2007), 58.

19. Evian Gordon, Kylie J. Barnett, Nicholas J. Cooper, Ngoc Tran and Leanne M. Williams, "An 'Integrative Neuroscience' Platform: Application to Profiles of Negativity and Positivity," *Journal of Integrative Neuroscience* 7 (2008) (3): 345–66.

20. David Rock and Linda J. Page, *Coaching with the Brain in Mind: Foundations for Practice* (Hoboken, NJ: John Wiley & Sons, 2009), 352–53, with reference to Daniel Goleman, *Emotional Intelligence: Why It Can Matter More Than IQ* (New York: Bantam Books, 1995).

21. *Ibid.*, 352.

22. *Ibid.*, 364.

23. *Ibid.*, 365.

24. *Ibid.*, 353.

25. Emily A. Butler and James J. Gross, "Hidden Feelings in Social Contexts: Out of Sight Is Not Out of Mind," Chapter 4 in Pierre Philippot and Robert S. Feldman, eds., *The Regulation of Emotion* (Mahwah, NJ: Lawrence Erlbaum Associates, 2004), 101–26.

26. James J. Gross and Oliver P. John, "Wise Emotion Regulation," Chapter 12 in Lisa Feldman Barrett, Peter Salovey and John D. Mayer, eds., *The Wisdom in Feeling: Psychological Processes in Emotional Intelligence* (New York: Guilford Press, 2002), 312–13.

27. From Roger Fisher and Daniel Shapiro, *Beyond Reason: Using Emotions as You Negotiate* (New York: Penguin Group, 2005), 228, referring to the discoveries and book by Joseph LeDoux, *The Emotional Brain: The Mysteries/Underpinnings of Emotional Life* (London: Weidenfield & Nicholson, 1998).

28. Daniel Goleman, *Destructive Emotions: A Scientific Dialogue with the Dalai Lama* (New York: Bantam, 2003).

29. Eileen Kennedy-Moore and Jeanne C. Watson, *Expressing Emotion: Myths, Realities, and Therapeutic Strategies* (New York: The Guilford Press, 1999) and Carol Tavris, *Anger: The Misunderstood Emotion* (New York: Simon & Schuster, 1989); cited by Roger Fisher and Daniel Shapiro, *Beyond Reason: Using Emotions as You Negotiate* (New York: Penguin Group, 2005), 229.

Client Engagement

The first part of this chapter deals with the inquiry stage—that is, the initial connections that coaches make with prospective clients and the referring person, when applicable. The second step in client engagement is the intake stage, which consists of various practices once the client decides to proceed with coaching. Both the inquiry and intake stages are familiar to coaches, mediators and others in the human services who screen and prepare people to participate in the pertinent forum. This chapter presents several key ideas of conflict management coaching, including the use of specific documents and forms that apply to these introductory steps. Although the concepts discussed here pertain to workplace coaching, most apply in other contexts as well, and the documents may be adapted accordingly.

Inquiry Stage

Objectives

Prospective clients,[1] and those who sponsor[2] or refer them to coaching, typically have some common objectives:

- To clarify what conflict management coaching is and how it works.
- To understand the respective roles of the coach, client and sponsor.
- To know the terms of the retainer, such as timing, duration, format and cost (when applicable).
- To find out about terms of confidentiality.

In addition to these and other initial queries, inquirers typically want to consider whether they "connect" with the coach as the right practitioner for them. The interaction during the inquiry stage similarly gives coaches the opportunity to consider whether they connect with the client. It is also a chance to assess any possible signs that the client or the objectives are not appropriate for coaching or the coach's practice.

Frequently Asked Questions

Coaches gain a lot of information about prospective clients and sponsors through the questions they ask in their initial communications. Because motivations are not always obvious, it is helpful for the coach to check out the reasons for the specific inquiry. Given the objectives listed above, what follows are the typical questions that clients and sponsors have at the inquiry stage. Some of these questions may arise later during the intake stage after a decision has been made to proceed.

- How does coaching work?
- What is the difference between coaching and therapy?
- How will I know if I am suited for coaching?
- Do I have to sign a contract?
- Is there a record kept in my employee (or other) file?
- How long are sessions?
- How long will coaching take?
- Do you use assessment tools?

Responses to these questions, and some reflections about the thinking behind them, follow. Some of the answers are specifically relevant to the CINERGY™ model of conflict management coaching. However, the essence of the responses may apply to other models, as well.

How Does Coaching Work?

Providing an understanding about what coaching is and how it works helps in many ways including to develop rapport with prospective clients and gain their trust. Also, most people embarking on the coaching process for the first time know little of how it works. Uncertainty about what is expected of them, and what to expect of the coach, may cause unnecessary anxiety.

Some people need to understand the specific process the coach uses. Under these circumstances, it helps to describe coaching as an informal conversation in which the coach uses strategic questioning and other skills in a step-by-step process aimed at helping clients reach their goals. An extensive explanation of the stages is not usually necessary at this point. Rather, a brief overview of what each step is intended to accomplish usually suffices and reassures prospective clients who value process and an understanding of the approach taken.

Conducting a short coaching session adds even more to this discussion, and is one of the best ways to demonstrate how coaching works. It also helps to ensure that clients know that the coach and client co-create the coaching relationship, and that together they will consider how things are progressing. This topic is discussed more later in this chapter and in Chapter 5.

To help support the conversation at this time, whether it occurs in person or by telephone, the coach may provide written information giving an overview on conflict management coaching, including a description of the roles of the coach and client. Figure 3.1 is an example of such an overview that has proven helpful in this initial discussion. A coaching agreement (Figure 3.3, later in this chapter) is also useful for informing prospective clients about what coaching entails and the respective roles.

FIGURE 3.1   THE CONFLICT MANAGEMENT COACHING RELATIONSHIP

What is conflict management coaching?

Conflict management coaching is a process in which a specially trained coach helps people on a one-on-one basis to improve the way they manage and interact in their interpersonal workplace conflicts and disputes. It is a future-oriented process that focuses on each person's specific conflict management goals. Conflict management coaching is not therapy or counseling.

What you can expect from your coach:

Besides helping you to reach your related goals, you can expect that I will provide you with constructive input and not judge you in any way. We will speak or meet on days and times that are mutually convenient. At these times I will use a step-by-step process aimed at keeping you focused on reaching your objectives. You can also expect that I will regularly check in with you to ensure you are progressing. My role is not to make decisions for you, to provide advice, or to act as your agent or representative.

What the coach expects from you:

I expect your willingness and honesty to share information about your conflict and goals. This includes your related concerns, expectations and needs. I also expect you will devote the time and energy to do the work required to achieve your objectives. A collaborative relationship is integral to the success of this process, and I anticipate we will both make our best efforts to co-create a mutually respectful and trusting working relationship. Along the way, if for any reason you have some discomfort with the process or me, please let me know so that we may discuss what may improve matters.

Tasks

It is often the case that clients work on some tasks between sessions. These tasks (or fieldwork, as I may refer to them) are meant to help you continue to move ahead toward your goals. Like other aspects of our relationship, we will work together about this aspect of coaching.

Thank you for stepping up to the coaching process. I look forward to working with you.

TASKS

After prospective clients have read an overview of the coaching process, they often ask about the last point on the subject of tasks. The role of tasks also known as fieldwork is discussed in Chapter 4, but for now, here are a few brief and relevant considerations.

Two of the coach's main expectations of clients are that they show up and that they step up. Showing up refers to being on time, being ready, being willing and committed to actively participate in the process and not repeatedly cancelling. Stepping up is about clients stretching themselves to optimize their potential by putting their energy into the work required to reach their objectives. Working on tasks between sessions is one of those ways.

Tasks are aimed at facilitating clients' progress between sessions and reflect their ongoing commitment to coaching. What clients work on depends on where they are in the coaching process at the end of each session, and any challenges or insights they may be experiencing. Tasks typically relate to what the client views as a way to move forward and may include what the coach also considers relevant and helpful. Informing prospective clients during the inquiry stage about fieldwork alerts them to how this aspect of coaching is integrated into the process and their lives.

What Is the Difference Between Coaching and Therapy?

Prospective clients often inquire whether coaching is counseling or therapy. Some may have misconceptions about these services or attach a stigma to those who use them. Coaching though it is neither counseling nor therapy does, however, have therapeutic elements. For instance, clients share their experiences with coaches who, like therapists and counselors, are caring, compassionate and thoughtful and who extend their undivided attention to them. Coaches, therapists and counselors all support people in their desire, quest and hope to improve some aspect of their personal or professional lives. While some forms of therapy—such as cognitive behavioral and solution-focused therapies—share some similar principles with coaching, there are differences in the processes used, the training of practitioners and other aspects of the work.

When prospective clients ask for clarification regarding this subject, comparing coaching to other processes such as therapy, counseling, consulting and mentoring helps to alleviate confusion and uncertainty. Comparisons may also clarify whether the prospective client might benefit from accessing a different service.

Appendix I outlines some commonalities and differences among coaching, consulting, therapy and mentoring. Though there is no necessity to go through detailed descriptions of these services, it is important for clients to know the main similarities and differences. The point to emphasize here is that coaching as a field of practice, and the particular model of conflict management coaching in this book, is different from counseling or therapy.

How Will I Know If I Am Suited for Coaching?

This question is also sometimes framed as, "What if I can't do this?" Clients who ask this may be insecure or uncertain about committing to the time required for coaching. They may also tend to be pessimistic, lack self-esteem, fear failure or demonstrate other self-limiting beliefs regarding their ability to make progress and succeed. Prospective clients may wonder about the efficacy of the coaching process, or may lack trust or confidence in themselves, the coach or the referring person.

The essence of "coaching readiness" is about being willing and able to commit to active participation in a future-oriented process aimed at making changes and reaching defined goals. Prospective clients who raise questions about their suitability for the process may wish to try a short quiz that helps them consider their readiness for coaching. Figure 3.2 is a sample questionnaire that addresses 10 possible criteria.

FIGURE 3.2   CONFLICT MANAGEMENT COACHING READINESS INDEX

Conflict management coaching is a specialized process aimed at helping individuals enhance the ways they manage and engage in conflict. Coaching requires a commitment of time and energy, and before beginning, it helps to check your level of readiness. Please circle the number that comes closest to representing how true each of the following 10 statements is for you at this time. Then, score yourself using the key at the bottom of the page. There is no right or wrong, and if the result is that you are not ready now, let's talk about what may facilitate your readiness.

Less True			More True		Statement
1	2	3	4	5	I have the strong intention of making my best efforts to gain more effective ways for engaging in conflict.
1	2	3	4	5	I am eager to increase my self-awareness and examine ways to change self-defeating behaviors that limit my ability to manage conflict more effectively.
1	2	3	4	5	I believe in my potential to be more effective regarding the way I react to and engage in conflict and am ready and willing to change things that do not serve others or me well.
1	2	3	4	5	I am open to considering how I contribute to conflict.
1	2	3	4	5	I am committed to being open and honest with the coach.
1	2	3	4	5	I am willing to do work during and between coaching sessions and be accountable for reaching my goals.
1	2	3	4	5	I am prepared to make the time and commitment to develop and take action steps to reach my goals.

Less True			More True		Statement
1	2	3	4	5	I understand that I am expected to do my own decision-making and that the coach's role is to provide the framework, process and support to facilitate my progress.
1	2	3	4	5	I understand that another of the coach's roles in supporting me is to provide observations. I welcome this type of input and will let the coach know how I best receive feedback.
1	2	3	4	5	If I am not getting what I need or expect from the coach or the process, I am willing to share this with the coach as soon as I experience any related dissatisfaction or concerns.

= TOTAL SCORE (Please add up the numbers chosen in each column and then total them. The scoring key is below.)

Scoring Key

10–20   I am not ready for conflict management coaching right now. *(If you still want to participate in coaching, let's talk about what might facilitate that happening.)*

21–30   I am ready for coaching, although I have some reservations or things that may hold me up. *(Let's make sure we talk about these before beginning.)*

31–40   I am ready for coaching and along with my coaching goals, will work on areas in this Index that indicate any lack of readiness.

41–50   I am very ready for coaching and along with my coaching goals, will work on the areas in this Index that indicate any lack of readiness.

Thank you. Please feel free to share areas that indicate lack of readiness.

Whether or not coaches use a questionnaire, when readiness is in question it helps to spend time with prospective clients to explore any factors of concern that may be coachable to facilitate their participation, if coaching is what they want. There are, of course, situations in which other interventions may be more appropriate. And some clients may simply not be ready or suited for conflict management coaching.

Do I Have to Sign a Contract?

Prospective clients who ask this question are often concerned about confidentiality. They may worry that information will be placed in their personnel file that could reflect on their career development. Or, they may question the legal implications of signing a contract.

Coaches contract verbally or in writing. Common provisions that constitute a professional coaching relationship include the coach's and client's roles and responsibilities, terms about confidentiality, voluntariness and logistics. Such conditions may be added to a document like the one in Figure 3.1, or be a part of a more formal agreement, such as the sample presented in Figure 3.3.

FIGURE 3.3   CONFLICT MANAGEMENT COACHING AGREEMENT

This is a Conflict Management Coaching Agreement made this _____ day of _____, 20___, between _____ , to be referred to as "the Client," and _____ , to be referred to as "the Coach."

The following is understood by us, as the basis for entering into our contract to work together:

1. Conflict Management Coaching

Conflict management coaching is a one-on-one process in which a trained coach helps people gain increased competence and confidence to manage their interpersonal conflicts and disputes. It is a future-oriented and voluntary process that focuses on each person's conflict management goals. Conflict management coaching is not therapy or counseling and in my role as your Coach, I will **not** provide advice or act as your agent or representative.

2. The Coach's Role

My primary role and responsibilities as your Coach are to:

- help you identify your goals and take the steps required to reach them;
- co-create a relationship with you that supports and facilitates your efforts to reach your goals;
- assist you to manage or resolve a dispute, or prevent one from escalating unnecessarily;
- help you strengthen your knowledge, skills and abilities to engage more effectively in conflict;
- manage the coaching process through the use of a step-by-step model designed to help you attain your objectives;
- help you explore any possible challenges to reaching your goals;
- provide honest observations and input that assist you in your efforts; and
- check in with you on a regular basis, to ensure you are progressing.

3. Your Role As Client

As Client, you agree to:

- communicate honestly with me;
- be willing to co-create our relationship and identify the best way we may collaborate to ensure that you progress;
- be open to my observations and input;
- commit the time and energy to fully participate;
- provide feedback to me on your experience of the coaching process and our working relationship;
- be accountable for doing the work required to reach your goals; and
- be solely responsible for your decisions and actions regarding your goals.

4. Confidentiality

As your Coach, I will maintain complete confidentiality about the content of the coaching sessions, unless:

- disclosure of the information is authorized by you, in writing;
- you reveal an intent to harm others or yourself;
- the information is required on an anonymous basis for educational or statistical purposes (no identifiable names and information are used); and
- required by applicable laws and court order.

5. Booking Sessions

We will schedule mutually convenient times to meet or speak, for up to ___ minutes up to ___ times per month for ___ months. We can then reassess together where you are at and determine whether you require more time.

If sessions need to be rescheduled, we both agree to provide the other with at least 24 hours' notice, if possible.

6. Voluntariness

Either of us may end the coaching process at any time before we have scheduled for it to end. If one of us decides to do so, he or she agrees to consider the optimum way to inform the other, which may include an explanation about the reasons.

Dated at _____ ,

this ___ day of _____ , 20____

_____   _____
Client: (name)   Coach: (name)

An agreement may contain additional terms about the coach's and client's shared responsibilities that reflect the concept of co-creating the working relationship. Examples of such provisions may include:

- To work together respectfully and thoughtfully.
- To both remain present throughout our time together.
- To reassess how to proceed if progress is not occurring.
- To trust the coaching process and ourselves within it.
- To embrace creativity, change, choice and possibilities.
- To accept that we may discover that we are not the appropriate fit for the work to be done and that it is no one's fault if that is the case.
- To accept feedback from each other in the spirit in which it is intended.
- To approach the coaching experience with optimism and positivity.

Contracts may additionally include fees and cancellation policies, depending on whether the client or sponsor is defraying the cost. (Contracting with sponsors is covered in more detail later in this chapter.) There are, of course, many other terms and wordings that coaches and clients may add. In any case, it is prudent for coaches to obtain legal advice to review the terms of any contracting document to be used, to ensure that appropriate terms for their practice are included.

Two components of the sample contract—confidentiality and voluntariness—deserve attention here because prospective clients often request clarification of these terms.

CONFIDENTIALITY

There is no privilege between coaches and clients. Coaches may be called upon to testify in a case initiated by a client or the client's organization that is pertinent to the subject matter of coaching. For instance, if a client is referred to coaching for inappropriate conduct in a conflict and is ultimately dismissed for repeated behaviors or lack of improvement, he or she may decide to bring a lawsuit for wrongful dismissal, and it is feasible the coach may be subpoenaed.

Conflict management coaching is not covered by the United States' *Alternative Dispute Resolution Act*. To date, no other statute is known to address confidentiality as it relates to coaching. Under these circumstances, conflict management coaching may be protected, to whatever extent possible, through a contracting document between the coach and client that provides a clear statement of the mutual intention about the confidentiality of their communications. Coaches' written policies and an applicable code of conduct further help support the intention regarding confidentiality. Contracts containing the terms of confidentiality signed by sponsors or otherwise acknowledged by them may also be used.

Other considerations regarding confidentiality, as they apply to workplace coaching, may include clarifying with the sponsor what constitutes reportable offenses that are not suitable for conflict management coaching. For example, some organizations require that individuals who admit or allege sexual harassment, discrimination and other civil rights breaches attend at an office or agency that specifically investigates the situation, to ensure that the violations are reported within the requisite period, if applicable. In this regard, some organizations (usually large private and public sector organizations) conduct a screening process to ensure prospective clients are aware that certain disclosures preclude confidentiality.[3] Another purpose of screening is to ensure that people are well informed of what coaching entails and what other services are available in the event that conflict management coaching is not a suitable forum.

Screening also helps to determine whether the conflict is more of a domestic nature. Domestic conflicts do not commonly fall within the purview of organizational conflict management coaches. If such disputes are raised by clients in the inquiry or intake stages, they are typically referred to an appropriate external or internal service, such as an Employee Assistance Program.

A topic related to confidentiality that sponsors often raise with coaches is about reporting on the progress of people they refer to coaching.* Some sponsors expect to be highly involved in working with the coach and client regarding the objectives, measuring success and monitoring the client's progress. On the other hand, some referring persons are minimally involved. They may expect that they will observe or hear whether coaching has produced affirmative results, and do not engage the coach in related conversation at any time. Typically, executive-level and other leaders participate in coaching with little, if any, intervention from the sponsor. There is a continuum, then, regarding the extent to which organizations are or want to be involved.

---

* It is important to add here that clients may retain external coaches independently of their organizations, or their workplaces may defray the expense. Increasingly, organizations have internal coaches on staff to provide coaching, as well.

Many coaches have specific practices with respect to how they interface with sponsors and clients. For this reason, it is necessary to have this conversation at the inquiry stage so that both sponsor and client are clear on this matter.

Because report writing is not a common practice, coaches usually have policies and procedures for communicating with sponsors who are actively involved in referring clients and want to monitor the staff member. Under these circumstances, one suggested format is for the coach, client and referring person to meet once it is confirmed that coaching is to proceed. The discussion may address the following topics:

- The anticipated outcome of coaching.
- How success will be measured.
- Terms relating to confidentiality.
- Duration of coaching.
- How progress will be shared.

If reporting back is requested, one viable practice is for the coach to meet with the referring person and the client at some point part-way through the timeframe allotted for coaching, at the end of coaching or at both times. At this point, a discussion on progress is usually based on the initially established measurement criteria and outcome expectations. This approach helps to meet the needs of the sponsors; it also supports the relationship between the coach and client, and allays the client's concerns about the possibility of private conversations between the coach and the sponsor.

VOLUNTARINESS

Voluntariness is another topic that often comes up in the inquiry stage when prospective clients read the word "voluntary" in the Conflict Management Coaching Agreement (Figure 3.3). Though many clients elect to see a coach and there is little to no involvement of the sponsor, others who are referred by supervisors, managers or HR professionals often ask, "How voluntary is voluntary?" A client who has been referred to participate in coaching because of problematic interactions and conflict conduct may react in ways that sidetrack the coaching conversation, at least temporarily. Under these circumstances, clients do not feel that they have any choice but to attend coaching. Concerns about voluntariness may also stem from fears that not participating will lead to retaliation on the part of the sponsor.

When resistance of any sort is evident, it is important for the coach to ask questions to gain an understanding of what it is about and possibly engage the client in an analysis of the possible risks and opportunities of proceeding. Coaches work through any reticence before coaching begins.

As coaching cultures continue to grow within organizations, and as effective conflict management is increasingly identified as a core competency, the benefits of individualized assistance gained through conflict management coaching will facilitate its acceptance as a developmental tool. It is also anticipated that referrals to coaching will not have the punitive implications that are sometimes associated with this intervention.

Of course, some clients will continue to have reservations about coaching, for other reasons. For example, choosing one's coach is not always feasible in organizations with only one internal coach, or when workplaces retain certain external coaches. These limitations mean that the client may not connect with the coach, or may resent or distrust the coach who is assigned. These, again, are matters that coaches routinely handle before coaching proceeds.

Another related question for discussion is whether the client is a good fit for the coach. This may be immediately apparent, or it may not arise until coaching has begun. Most coaches instinctively sense whether there are potential challenges that may preclude their continuing. Lack of comfort with clients' energy and attitude, a sense that their respective values do not align and clashes in other ways may occur such that coaches question their own suitability. Any apprehensions that a client is not appropriate for the coach require the practitioner to explore and clarify the dynamic.

Other reasons that lead coaches to decline proceeding include the discovery that the client's issues are beyond their expertise or that they are ethically challenged because of a conflict of interest.

Is There a Record Kept in My HR (or Other) File?

Questions about record keeping and storage are usually related to concerns over confidentiality. Clients who ask this question are typically concerned about what might appear in their personnel records and whether the fact or substance of coaching may be revealed. Fears may prevail that referral to coaching may reflect negatively on clients' performance, career advancement and developmental opportunities. Access-to-information legislation in some countries adds to concerns about the availability of written notes.

Coaches' notes, like coach–client communications, are not privileged, and practices for taking and storing them vary. Some coaches keep their notes; others give them to their clients, or shred them in front of them, after coaching is over. Others keep non-identifiable notes or other documents that indicate the number and duration of sessions.

Policies and procedures regarding storage of records kept by internal coaches are set by the organization and the practitioners and consider any related laws. In any case, transparency is crucial in these matters.

How Long Are Sessions?

This common question seems straightforward. But sometimes it relates to clients' anxieties about getting their work done or being noticed as absent from the workplace and unavailable when needed for certain periods of time. Some clients may have medical problems or an attention deficit and are hesitant to say so. Reluctance about making a commitment to coaching may also be behind this query.

Coaches will want to provide information on their usual scheduling practices and be as flexible as possible in responding to clients' concerns and the task at hand. Sessions vary in length for a variety of reasons. Most coaches, however, set aside specific periods of time and intervals for sessions in collaboration with their clients. Common practice averages 30 to 60 minutes on a weekly basis.

Coaches remain conscious of clients' energy levels and attention spans and are careful to not overload them. Also, if clients are highly emotional in sessions, they may require more time to process their feelings. In the initial research for developing the CINERGY™ model, most study group members reported that 50 to 60 minutes was their limit for being able to concentrate during sessions. Experience suggests that setting aside 60 minutes helps in scheduling and managing time, although specific circumstances may shorten or lengthen some sessions. Winding down each session with five to 10 minutes at the end provides an opportunity to discuss reflections, the ongoing schedule and tasks for moving forward before the next meeting.

A pertinent topic that coaches may wish to raise in the inquiry stage, if the prospective client does not, is the format that will be used for the coaching sessions. Face-to-face, telephone and computer-based communication are all common formats for coaching. Even when the coach and client live in the same city, it is not always practical to meet in person. Discussing alternative ways to connect and the related costs is part of this conversation.

How Long Will Coaching Take?

Duration of coaching is specific to each client's objectives; it is not easy to state explicitly how many sessions it will take for clients to reach them.

Prospective clients may ask this question out of straightforward curiosity. However, sometimes clients ask this question because they are apprehensive about their situation, the coaching process or both. They may have limited commitment to coaching or feel pressure—internal or external—to get things "sorted out" expeditiously. Some people have a tendency to take action hurriedly and push ahead without patience or thought. Or, there may be other reasons that reflect reluctance. Whatever the reason is, it likely presents a coachable opportunity to assist clients with their related anxieties. Sometimes when this question arises, coaches may need to ensure that clients understand that conflict management coaching is not a "quick fix."

Given that the factors for determining duration are variable, it is unrealistic for clients to expect to make substantial progress in one or two sessions. Though many people may be able to make some changes in a short time, it is prudent to discuss expectations as a starting point in the inquiry stage.

Some organizations have policies that limit the number of sessions for internal coaching,[4] and budgetary reasons often prevail when external coaches are contracted. Other variables include whether the conflict is a single dispute or a series of disputes. If the coaching is intended to develop conflict competence rather than manage a specific dispute, the duration is typically longer.

Do You Use Assessment Tools?

A question about the use of assessment tools is often about how progress and success will be evaluated. Sponsors are more likely to ask this question rather than prospective clients.

Many organizations routinely use tools to assess a range of traits and characteristics, including conflict behaviors and communication skills. Depending on the relevance to the client's objectives and the coach's certification with respect to the instrument, the results may be used in conflict management coaching. On the other hand, instruments that are specifically designed to assess conflict-related styles and responses may be preferable.

If this question is raised in the inquiry stage, the coach has an opportunity to describe any assessment tools typically used and the additional costs.

The need for an assessment may, however, not be apparent until coaching begins. The choice of appropriate instrument or whether designing a new one is required are further considerations. Chapter 7 discusses assessment tools in greater detail.

Intake Stage

The intake stage occurs once the client and coach establish that coaching will proceed. The first coaching session may follow right after intake, depending on the client and the situation. In other cases, intake is a separate, initial meeting for the express purpose of having a comprehensive, preparatory discussion.

Objectives

The coach's main objectives at the intake stage, depending on the level of inquiry that has already taken place, include:

- To build upon the rapport initiated in the inquiry stage.
- To provide information about the coaching model, if not previously discussed.
- To ensure that clients understand what coaching is and is not.
- To ensure that clients understand their role and responsibilities and those of the coach.
- To discuss the client's readiness, based on the Conflict Management Coaching Readiness Index (Figure 3.2).
- To review and sign an agreement, such as the Conflict Management Coaching Agreement (Figure 3.3).
- To confirm any limits on topics for coaching.
- To schedule dates and duration of appointments and coaching.
- To confirm the format of coaching.
- To confirm the terms of the retainer.
- To prepare the client for the first session.
- To respond to the client's questions.

Building and sustaining the client–coach connection is described in greater detail in Chapter 5. What follows here are several other points related to the intake stage.

Confirm the Terms of the Retainer

Coaches may be retained in several ways. External coaches may draft an agreement or a retainer letter, or submit a formal proposal that is subject to written or oral confirmation by the sponsor or individual client. Internal coaches may also enter into written agreements according to terms agreed to by the coach, client and sponsor, when involved. A contract such as the Conflict Management Coaching Agreement (Figure 3.3) may be used, or another document that confirms the arrangement.

Figure 3.4 shows a sample retainer letter by an external coach to a sponsor. This document sets up an initial and subsequent meeting among the external coach, the referring person and the client; other arrangements may differ and, for instance, not include such meetings. A retainer letter may be adapted for direct engagement with clients, and other clauses may be added pertaining to applicable disbursements, such as an assessment tool, parking, mileage and so on.

FIGURE 3.4   SAMPLE RETAINER LETTER BY AN EXTERNAL COACH TO A SPONSOR

Hello, Ms. Brooke:

This letter is further to our meeting on _____ , at which time you confirmed that your organization is retaining me to provide coaching for _____ , for the reasons conveyed to him and me when we all met on _____.

The following confirms the terms of my retainer, as discussed:

- I will provide my services for ____ for ____ months and for up to a total of ____ hours during this timeframe. The number of hours includes in-person, telephone or email communications with ____ docketed during this period and the review meeting you requested.

- The timeframe begins _____ and ends _____ , subject to a further extension which as discussed, will be one of the considerations at a review meeting with you, ____ and myself on or before _____. As also discussed, my office will coordinate the date and time of this meeting.

- It is further understood that prior to our review meeting or when coaching is scheduled to end, the organization, the staff member being coached or I may call an end to the coaching relationship in accordance with clause 6 of the attached agreement.* Any outstanding fees or those unbilled for time provided when the relationship ends, remain the responsibility of the organization.

- The hourly fee for the above period is ____ to be invoiced on the last business day of each month and is payable by the organization within ____ days, after which interest is charged at the rate of ____%.

- Appointments cancelled by the client within ____ hours will be invoiced as ____ minutes.

- The terms of confidentiality are in accordance with clause 4 of the attached coaching agreement* which will be signed by _____ and me. It is understood by this agreement that the content of the communications between _____ and me remain confidential subject to the relevant clauses.

Your signature below will confirm that the above summary accurately reflects the terms of my retainer. If not, please otherwise advise me in writing of any changes or additions you would like.

Thank you for this opportunity to work with _____ and do not hesitate to contact me if there are any questions.

With appreciation,

_____   _____
Mr. Coach   Ms. M. Brooke

---

  * The Conflict Management Coaching Agreement (Figure 3.3) is not duplicated here.

Preparing the Client for the First Session

Once the terms of the retainer are confirmed, and depending on how soon the coaching process begins, a common practice is to ask the client to consider some aspects of coaching in advance of the first session. Figure 3.5 gives an example of the types of questions that the coach may use for this purpose.

FIGURE 3.5   PREPARING FOR YOUR FIRST COACHING SESSION

I look forward to getting to know you and helping you reach your objectives. To prepare you for our first coaching session, the following will help build the foundation for our work together. Your responses are CONFIDENTIAL between us.

Because coaching works best when clients have clear goals, please identify what you are hoping to achieve in conflict management coaching:

_____

_____

_____

Please let me know, too:

- What is motivating you most at this time, to obtain coaching?

_____

_____

- How will you measure whether coaching is effective for you?

_____

_____

- How do you expect your manager, reports, co-workers and others will know that conflict management coaching is effective for you?

_____

_____

- What is the optimum way for me to provide my feedback and observations to you during our coaching relationship?

_____

_____

_____

- How do you usually get focused to be able to concentrate on a task?

_____

_____

_____

- What do you want to know or understand about coaching, and how the process works, that you don't know yet?

_____

_____

_____

- What else do you want me to know about you?

_____

_____

_____

- What do you want to know about me?

_____

_____

_____

Thank you for taking the time to answer the above questions. If possible, please send your responses to me in advance of our first meeting.

Fax: _____   Email: _____

If you have any questions before we begin, please do not hesitate to contact me.

A document such as this outlines the preliminary work that helps prepare clients to begin to share information about themselves and to focus their intentions. It also gives clients an opportunity to start thinking about their expectations and hopes for the coaching process and the working relationship with the coach. Reviewing the answers together at the first session helps the coach and client get to know each other, build rapport and co-create the relationship.

Other pertinent questions that may be added or form part of the initial one-on-one coaching conversation include the following:

- Generally, how would you describe the way you manage conflict at this time?
- What do you do well when you are in conflict?
- How do you prefer to be and be seen with respect to how you engage in conflict?
- How do you describe the way that conflict is addressed in your team?
- How would you describe the corporate culture of your workplace when it comes to managing conflict (communication, etc.)?

Further possible questions might focus on the coach–client relationship:

- What do people say or do that demonstrates that you are being supported?
- When you perceive you are being listened to—what is the listener doing or saying that works best for you?
- In what ways would you like you and me to be able to rely on each other in our working relationship?
- What ideas do you have about how we might best work together?

SUMMARY

- Many prospective clients have no experience with coaching and no clear idea about how it works. It is therefore important for the coach to anticipate their questions to ensure that they are well informed about conflict management coaching. Providing written information, answering their questions, conducting a short coaching session and generally being transparent about all aspects of the process are all components of effective client engagement.

- Not everyone is ready, willing and able to engage in coaching. It is important that prospective clients are committed to engage in the coaching process and have the time, energy and openness to make changes in their lives. The inquiry stage is the time at which to assess the client's readiness and to initiate a discussion about what may be needed to proceed.

- Prospective clients and referring sponsors will want to ensure that the coach is the right one for them and their organization. The coach, too, will want to determine whether the fit is appropriate or whether the client requires an alternative service or coach.

- Conflict management coaching requires a supportive milieu and working relationship between coach and client. The synergy, trust and rapport that coaches aim to build early on and throughout the process help to instill comfort and motivation for clients to actively participate in the process.

- Clarification of roles and responsibilities of the client, the sponsor and the coach is imperative for client engagement. It is also necessary to ensure that prospective clients are informed about what coaching is and what it is not.

- Preliminary steps in advance of coaching, such as how best to work together, help prepare clients to engage in the process and ensure that they begin to consider and set their intentions early on.

- The inquiry and intake stages of client engagement frequently overlap. Once clients commit to proceed with coaching, some kind of formal agreement, whether written or oral, establishes the coaching relationship. The agreement touches on such matters as confidentiality, voluntariness, logistics and other related provisions. Ensuring that clients and sponsors are clear on all aspects of contracting is a necessary part of client engagement.

Notes

1. The definition of "client" by the International Coach Federation is used here and refers to "the person being coached."

2. The definition of "sponsor" by the International Coach Federation is used here and refers to the "entity (including its representatives) paying for and/or arranging for the provision of coaching services." The expressions "referring person" and "sponsor" will be used interchangeably in this book.

3. See, for instance, Cinnie Noble, Sam Slosberg and Scott Becker, "Conflict Management Coaching at the Transportation Security Administration," *Mediate.com*, October 2009: http://www.mediate.com/articles/nobleC11.cfm.

4. *Ibid.*

The CINERGY™ Conflict Coaching Model

A conceptual model offers a framework for synthesizing knowledge based on experience and observation. This chapter presents the stages of the CINERGY™ model, as developed with the active participation of a study group (see Introduction), for coaching individuals through conflict. The intention of each stage of the model is explained along with suggestions that support coaches in their use of this framework.

The Value of Having a Model

As the study group that helped develop the CINERGY™ model progressed along the continuum from their starting point toward their conflict management goals, it became evident that a relatively structured and methodical process kept them focused and directed. Based on the group's feedback and experiences, what emerged is a staged approach that provides a compass and roadmap for helping clients move forward, each stage building on the one that precedes it. This step-by step approach, giving clients sufficient time to think and feel what each stage offers, is key to using this model and supporting clients' journey of discovery, change and growth.

Though coaches who use the CINERGY™ model follow the steps, they are also comfortable following clients to the other places they go in their thoughts and emotions as they move through the process. Coaches know too when and how to bring clients back to the model to further their progress and goal attainment. Robert and Dorothy Bolton explain the concept of a model that resonates with this approach and the intentions of the CINERGY™ framework:

> *An elegant model is a useful simplification of reality.* It enables you to ignore a mass of irrelevant or less relevant details so you can focus on what is most important. A model shows what to look for, helps identify meaningful patterns, and aids in interpreting what you see. In other words, a model helps cut through the distracting aspects of a situation so you can better grasp the essence of what you want to understand.[1]

Stages and Intentions of the CINERGY™ Model

Being clear on the intentions of each of the seven stages assists coaches using the CINERGY™ model (Figure 4.1).

FIGURE 4.1   STAGES AND INTENTIONS
OF THE CINERGY™ MODEL

	Stage	Intentions
C	Clarify the Goal	• To determine what the client wants to achieve in coaching.
I	Inquire About the Situation	• To hear what interaction(s) precipitated the conflict or dispute • To let the client vent • To clarify with whom the client is in conflict
N	Name the Elements	• To help the client deconstruct the elements of conflict to (a) increase the client's self-awareness and (b) consider the other person's viewpoint • To have the client identify and reflect on any new awareness, insights and perspectives, based on deconstructing the conflict • To have the client reassess the goal, having deconstructed the situation and gained different views
E	Explore Choices	• To help the client explore possibilities for a plan of action to reach the stated goal • To help the client consider the risks and opportunities of the possible choices
R	Reconstruct the Situation	• To have the client confirm a choice, or select the order of choices, to develop as a plan of action • To coach the client to create, reconstruct, rehearse and prepare options for reaching the goal. This involves (a) confirming the client's desired outcome of the choice selected, (b) setting up situations for the client to test and examine and (c) providing effective feedback and observations to the client, who practices new skills consistent with his or her goal and outcome
G	Ground the Challenges	• To consider any challenges that may impede the client's plan, once it is confirmed
Y	Yes, the Commitment	• To confirm the client's next steps • To hear the client's learnings ("takeaways") • To discuss a task for moving forward • To acknowledge the client's efforts and end on a positive note

The section that follows describes the stages of the CINERGY™ model in more detail and offers some considerations about the intentions of each step. Two important points here are that (1) it takes more than one session to go through the model and to do justice to its incremental nature, and (2) clients often take "sideways" journeys that may need to be explored.

Clarify the Goal

> ## *Intention*
> To determine what the client wants to achieve in coaching

Knowing what motivates people to seek conflict management coaching is key to helping them get there. As in most coaching models, the client's goal essentially drives the process and is a starting point of the coaching conversation. Clarifying what clients want to accomplish keeps them and the coach on track. By asking clients to express their purpose when the process begins, coaches ensure that their expectations, hopes and vision remain in the forefront.

The possibilities for goals are limitless. Some examples in conflict management coaching might be:

- To talk to my co-worker about a matter before going to our boss.
- To see how I can stop the ongoing tension I am experiencing with my co-worker about the disagreement we had.
- To be less accommodating on this project.
- To stop avoiding a difficult conversation I have to have with my staff member.
- To figure out why I reacted so strongly in that situation.
- To prepare for a mediation.

- To mend a relationship that is having a negative impact on my work.
- To think more about whether to just let the argument pass, or to say something else to resolve things.
- To not react defensively with my manager.

Asking clients what they want to accomplish in coaching might seem a simple question. Certainly, many are able to articulate their goal immediately and clearly. However, some clients may have difficulty imagining a goal. Others who have been referred to coaching may not understand the reasons for the referral or how a coach might assist them. For instance, a sponsor may say, "You need help with that argument you had with Karl. Why don't you see a coach?" Or, "I want you to see the coach, Mary. You have to stop being so aggressive and stop arguing with everyone!" The importance of ascertaining the goal as the first step cannot be overstated. Its significance becomes more evident as the process unfolds.

There are a number of facets to clarifying goals. What follows are some considerations about the intention of the "C" stage.

CLIENTS MAY NEED TIME TO IDENTIFY GOALS

When we are in conflict, we may react in a range of ways depending on variables like the degree of hurt, our ability to regulate our emotions, who the other person is, the circumstances, the stakes, our personal rule book, our habitual style of interacting when provoked and so on. Some people act impulsively; others withdraw; some yell; some respond with blame. However, by the time many people come to conflict management coaching, their initial strong feelings about the situation and the other person may have subsided. With the lapse of time or having retold their story numerous times, much of the related anger and intensity may be reduced. Other clients may remain preoccupied and upset by the incident that has led them to seek the help of a conflict coach. High emotions may continue to prevail or be renewed when they meet with the coach.

Sometimes clients have not yet thought through what they are hoping to achieve, or they may be unable to consider their goal as yet. If initial answers to the question about their objectives are "I don't know" or "I'm not sure," the coach can simply offer the client more time and space. When clients reflect more and understand that the process starts with the end in mind, they are usually able to name their goals.

CONSIDERING GOALS IN ADVANCE IS GOOD COACHING PRACTICE

Asking clients to consider their goals before beginning coaching primes them to clarify what they hope to accomplish. They begin to focus on what is important to them and what they want to happen. They also have an opportunity to concentrate their attention and commitment to the first steps of their participation in the process.

The questions in Figure 3.5 (Preparing for Your First Coaching Session, Chapter 3, page 104) ask clients to identify what they hope to achieve in conflict management coaching and how they will measure its effectiveness. Most clients who complete this type of document (or who consider verbal questions of this nature) in advance of coaching report that it helps them contemplate their expectations if they have not already done so. When clients are referred to coaching, and when sponsors are involved (see Chapter 3), goals are typically discussed in an initial meeting before coaching starts.

THERE MAY BE A NUMBER OF DIFFERENT GOALS

Goal-setting helps manage expectations because some clients have objectives that are unrealistic, both in nature and in timeframe. For instance, consider the client Serena, who comes to the first session with three unrelated goals she hopes to reach in one session. She may have unrealistic expectations and may lack knowledge about what coaching is and how it works. Or, stress and anxiety to get matters resolved may be having an impact on her. Possibly, Serena has a tendency to make snap decisions without thinking them through, reflecting old habits about how she usually manages conflict situations.

It is common in conflict management coaching that clients come with both short- and long-term goals. Short-term goals are often related to a specific dispute that has happened, is in progress or is anticipated—for example, "to figure out how to present a difficult issue at the staff meeting that is bound to create conflict" or "to make amends with Joe about our argument." Even "to figure out what to do about an argument I had" is an example of a short-term objective. Longer-term goals are usually less dispute-specific and are more about general ways of coping: "to learn better ways of responding to criticism," or "to figure out how to work more effectively with people who are aloof."

Determining the starting point and assisting clients to develop a plan about their priorities are part of the initial stage of the CINERGY™ model when clients present several goals. When coaches help clients define their immediate objectives and "chunk" the work into more manageable pieces, the work ahead is more focused and less daunting for them.

CONFLICT MANAGEMENT COACHING MAY NOT BE THE APPROPRIATE FORUM

Another rationale for clarifying the goal at the beginning is to ensure that clients understand what conflict management coaching is and the coach's role. For instance, goals such as "I want to have someone fired," "I want them to change that stupid policy," "I've got to leave this organization" or "I want to kibosh a plan so no one succeeds" all require further explanation as to what the client expects and to determine whether the goal is within the coach's purview (or, for that matter, is ethical). Sometimes, though, an initial statement may only seem to fall outside the coach's role. Consider Mac's goal, "To get out of this organization." It sounds like he needs career coaching or help other than conflict management coaching. However, upon further questioning, Mac may reveal that he wants assistance initiating a conversation with his boss about a contentious workplace situation that compels him to want to leave.

As suggested in Chapter 3, some situations are unsuitable for coaching. Accusations or admissions of sexual harassment are usually referred to appropriate offices as a first step of addressing such matters. Similarly, in cases of domestic conflict, internal and external coaches who help with interpersonal workplace disputes typically refer employees to Employee Assistance Programs or other services that handle personal matters. Yet, conflict management coaching can be used for these and other issues, depending on the policies of the organization and the coach's level of expertise. It is important that coaches inform clients and sponsors, before coaching starts, about what is and is not within the coach's purview. If there was no screening process prior to coaching beginning, or if the coach's role and scope were not clearly understood at the inquiry or intake stages, this step serves to ensure the objectives fit the forum.

One further point about suitability: some organizations view coaching as part of corrective or disciplinary action. While this approach may suit some coaches, others may prefer to stay away from matters that can potentially result in a grievance, lawsuit or other forum requiring them to testify. This topic warrants mention here because coaches may not become aware of the background until coaching begins and not realize that the client's goal is not appropriate for their practice. Providing sufficient information in the inquiry stage, and asking pertinent questions before confirming that coaching is to proceed, are safeguards for coaches who prefer not to take on certain situations.

GOALS MAY CHANGE

Many clients are clear on their coaching objectives at the beginning and maintain them throughout the process. It is possible, however, that a client's goal may change. As the process unfolds, coaches listen to whether clients are moving away from their stated purpose and check in with them if that happens. This commonly happens at the "N" stage, though it may occur at other times as the process unfolds. Shifts in goals often occur as clients gain increased insight into their conflicts and the dynamics between them and the other person.

As clients become more comfortable in the space coaches co-create with them, many possibilities typically unfold that were not available or accessible to them earlier. When a goal does change, it may expand, contract or shift altogether. Acknowledging to clients at the beginning that their goal may change, or become clearer, reassures those who are uncertain about their objectives.

CLIENTS MAY NEED TO VENT FIRST

When coaches ask about clients' objectives in this beginning stage, some immediately pour out what happened in their conflict or dispute. This tends to occur with people whose emotions are running high. They are anxious to vent and share their view of what happened. Some may not yet have expressed their feelings about their situation, or they may have told others but did not feel heard. That means that some clients may be unable to focus on their goal in the "C" stage until they have vented about their situation and the accompanying emotions.

Coaches generally tend to listen more specifically to what a client recounts in the "I" stage because it applies to the goal when they know what has motivated the person to seek coaching. That is, knowing the client's goal helps coaches to filter out extraneous information and check relevance when the information being communicated appears unrelated to the stated objective. However, it is the client's journey, and it is important that the coach be where the client is.

MAKE NO ASSUMPTIONS

A cautionary comment to coaches on clients' goal-setting is to be aware of any tendency to reframe or rephrase how clients express their goals. Sometimes clients may struggle at first to articulate their objectives, and it is important that coaches do not speak for them. This is the case even if coaches perceive they are rephrasing or reframing based on the client's words. The coach's interpretation may inadvertently limit and even distort the client's intention. For example, a client's goal expressed as, "I think I need to talk to Karen about an argument we had" does not translate into, "You want to make amends with Karen." The client may not consider making amends as an objective. Rather, the objective may be to let Karen know the impact of her constant competitiveness and the client's request for her to stop.

Further, clients at this juncture have not necessarily thought out an outcome of their goal. Experience suggests it is not a good use of time to go into the outcome of the client's goal just yet. Clients' ultimate objectives, and how to achieve them, are more meaningfully discussed in the "E" and "R" stages after they have had the opportunity to analyze the elements of their conflict or dispute in the "N" stage of the CINERGY™ model.

GOALS ARE MEASURES OF SUCCESS AND KEEP CLIENTS AND COACHES ON TRACK

Clarity of the goal not only keeps clients focused, purposeful and intentional. Their stated objectives are coaches' goalposts used throughout coaching to gauge progress according to what each client is aiming to achieve. Identifying the specific goal, and any changes that evolve, serves to frame the criteria by which clients, sponsors and coaches measure success of coaching.

Inquire About the Situation

> ### *Intention 1*
> To hear what interaction(s) precipitated the conflict or dispute

This is the stage in which coaches simply ask the client to describe what happened. Clients will typically choose the incident or series of interactions that resulted in their seeking or being referred to coaching. If there was a precipitating event in the client's history with the other person that predated the current conflict, clients commonly recount that as well or instead. At this time, it is important just to let clients express their version of what occurred between them and the other person. Coaches using this model listen for the pertinent elements of conflict that will be more fully explored in the "N" stage and so do not probe in any depth at this juncture.

Some other points to consider about the intention of this part of CINERGY™ model follow.

THE FACTS ABOUT CONFLICTS ARE NOT COMMONLY THE FOCUS

Chapter 2 talked about how people often embellish or distort their conflicts to suit their self-interests when retelling what occurred. Interpretations of what happened often tend to be perceived as factual realities. Also, clients sometimes leave out information and mix what they wish they had said with what they actually said. The significance of such factors as they relate to clients' conflict narratives is multifold.

Here are some considerations regarding "facts":

- It is usually not necessary to examine details of the facts of the conflict. These are typically not as relevant to clients' goals as are the particular actions or words that created their emotional responses.
- Unlike mediation and other processes where there are issues in dispute that the parties want to resolve, people do not typically consult a conflict management coach with the same objective. However, if this is the case, it will be evident by what the client conveys, and the need to clarify the related facts will emerge.
- Questions motivated by curiosity about the facts can be time-wasting and take the coach and the client away from the objective of coaching.
- Before engaging clients in discussion about what they are sharing in this stage, it helps for coaches to ask themselves, "What is the relevance of this question to the client's goal?"

COACHES REQUIRE IMPARTIALITY ABOUT THE "OTHER PERSON"

It is not the place of the coach to judge the client's perception of the conflict or of the other person in the dispute. It also helps to keep in mind that there are two and sometimes more sides to every story. This means that it is important for coaches to remain impartial about the other person(s) involved in the client's conflict.

Though coaches support and empathize with their clients, if they give the impression or make the assumption that the client's version accurately describes the full picture, there is a risk that the client will be reticent about admitting his or her contribution to the conflict. By remaining open to and non-judgmental about this possibility, coaches facilitate clients' comfort to share truths about their part in the conflict, which they might otherwise hesitate to disclose in the "N" stage, when a deeper exploration considers both sides of the situation.

Intention 2
To let the client vent

Some things to consider about the intention of this part of the "I" stage follow.

COACHES' EMPATHY AND LISTENING SKILLS FACILITATE CLIENTS' SHARING

Clients want coaches to believe them. Depending on a wide range of factors, they may also want to justify their actions, take blame away from themselves, have the coach legitimize their perceptions, be seen as a victim, gain sympathy and so on.

This part of the "I" stage is one of the many times in the model that the coach's silence is necessary, and that clients have space to talk out their perceptions without interruption. Paying close attention to them—empathizing and acknowledging the impact of their situation—goes a long way in letting clients know they are being heard.

Coaches also listen for what else is happening with clients beyond their descriptions of the conflict-related event(s) and refrain from a tendency to explore details.

PEOPLE SHOW EMOTIONS AND SHARE INFORMATION DIFFERENTLY

Even if the intensity of their emotions has subsided by the time of the first session, many clients want to share the impact of their conflict. Coaches know that people show emotions and share information in different ways. As discussed in Chapter 2 in the part about emotions, some clients emote a lot, some very little and some appear uncertain about how much to share. Clients' state of mind and heart varies, of course, according to whatever is going on for them about the situation at the time and their particular way of coping and expressing themselves. Habitual ways of communicating, not wanting to be perceived as a complainer, tendencies to suppress emotions, fear of crying and other reasons account for the way and degree to which people communicate their emotional experience of conflict.

Other variables have an impact on the amount of information and degree of emotion that some clients are willing to share. For instance, they may feel they are just getting to know the coach and may not yet trust him or her, or the terms of confidentiality. The process of coaching may also foster fears of failure, insecurities and other feelings of vulnerability and uncertainty. It may sometimes take several sessions for clients to reveal relevant data and emotions. In any case, the "N" stage of the model will elicit more defined information, and it helps to keep this in mind.

THERE IS A FINE BALANCE ABOUT HOW MUCH VENTING IS HELPFUL

Many clients find that telling the coach about their conflict is a cathartic experience, unlike times they have talked to others about their situation. For instance, clients commonly report that family and friends rush to give advice, make light of what occurred, personalize the situation or provide other less than helpful responses. Some say that talking to a coach is the first time that a person listened to them non-judgmentally without interruption, empathized with them and validated their pain. Extending time and attentive listening gives clients who are willing the chance to say and feel what is in their minds and in their hearts.

After venting, most clients become increasingly ready to move ahead in the coaching process. However, if they seem unable to turn from their hurts to begin to work toward their goals, this is an important signal for coaches to ask what is holding them in the quagmire of their conflict. As suggested in Chapter 2, venting has the potential for causing a negative and pessimistic mood that keeps clients in the depths of what upsets them. Further, they may come to the session ruminating about their situation, and moving ahead may seem daunting at this time. They may be angry at or unforgiving of themselves. These and variations of how emotions affect people in conflict, including brain chemistry, are factors that coaches may encounter in this stage.

Checking with clients about their readiness to move on is a delicate balance. (Chapter 5 deals with this topic in greater detail.) Coaches remain aware of the need to support a client's venting and at the same time, contemplate the possible consequences of dwelling on the past with all the associated despair, blame, anger, hurt and so on. There is also the matter of managing clients' expectations with respect to what they are hoping to achieve and the extent to which coaches are able to assist them. Given the future-oriented nature of coaching, the timeframe allocated for sessions and the related reality check regarding progress, it is the role of the coach to know how and when to test clients' readiness to move forward. All these factors are important considerations for coaches that require them to listen carefully and compassionately to where clients are coming from and assure them they are being heard.

Experience helps coaches determine when it is time to transition into the "N" stage, where they assist clients to break down their conflicts into more manageable chunks and view them with a more cognitive and less emotional lens. Experience also informs coaches when clients are not ready, or when it is time to discuss whether coaching is the appropriate service.

NOT EVERYONE NECESSARILY WANTS TO VENT

Many clients process their emotions about their conflict in their own way before coming to coaching. They may be ready to engage in the process and will not want or be expected to express their emotions about what happened. There is no necessity to push clients to share what they do not want to share. If it becomes apparent that unresolved feelings may be driving decisions that are contrary to clients' goals or impeding their progress, coaches can share their observations with the client at that time.

Intention 3

To clarify with whom the client is in conflict

It is common for clients to state the name of the other person in either the "C" or "I" stage. When they do not do so, it is important to ask for one, even a fictionalized name. For example, clients concerned about confidentiality may be reluctant to reveal the name of someone whom an internal coach may know.

Further, sometimes clients refer to the other person in pejorative ways ("this idiot," "that whiner," "this trouble-maker" and so on). By asking for a name, coaches reduce the inherent dehumanizing or objectifying that name-calling breeds, and they avoid implicitly agreeing with the client's judgments. However, negative references can serve as coachable occasions. When clients identify the other person in derogatory ways, those names often reflect clients' emotions, and asking for an explanation of these terms opens up the related conversation.

Name the Elements

Intention 1

To help the client deconstruct the elements of conflict/dispute to (a) increase the client's self-awareness and (b) consider the other person's viewpoint

---

In the "N" stage, the conflict or dispute is broken down (deconstructed) into its various elements according to the (Not So) Merry-Go-Round of Conflict (Figure 4.2), the schematic introduced in Chapter 2 based on the common pathways people in conflict follow once they are provoked. Methodically following the sequence of this analysis in the "N" stage is pivotal for helping clients examine the cognitive, emotional, relational and behavioral lenses inherently contained within the merry-go-round. This schematic not only reflects the common trajectory that unpacks the elements of the conflict for clients. It also helps clients gain different perspectives, including *mutuality*—what happens when clients imagine themselves in the other person's shoes and analyze what appeared to happen for him or her.

Within the context of Figure 4.2, then, the line of inquiry in this stage starts with the client's perceptions of the elements that comprise the conflict. Coaches ask the client to fully consider his or her perspective on each element. In practice, this essentially means asking the client the series of questions posed to readers in Chapter 2 where the merry-go-round analysis was described. After exploring the elements from the client's perspective, coaches then ask the client to mentally walk along the same pathway with the same line of inquiry and consider the other person's possible perspective. This method for helping clients gain self-awareness and a sense of mutuality works effectively for many reasons:

- The (Not So) Merry-Go-Round of Conflict takes the dynamics of conflict out of a "blame frame" and into the realm of

FIGURE 4.2   The (Not So) Merry-Go-Round of Conflict

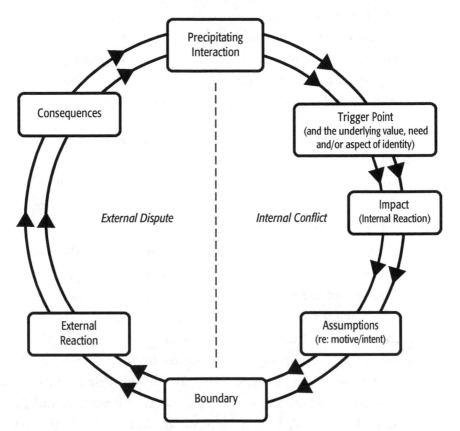

what may be described as a pathway that people commonly follow when involved in interpersonal conflict.

- By paying close attention to each specific element of the situation, clients gain increased understanding and awareness of themselves and the other person in conflict.
- Considering that the other person's trajectory consists of the same elements that the client experienced tends to foster empathy and clarify what happened in more objective ways.
- The notion that people generally follow a common conflict pathway when they react negatively to the deeds and words of others tends to normalize conflict.

- Looking at conflicts and disputes in this way helps clients reflect on their contribution to the dynamic in a way that reduces defensiveness and misplaced emotions.
- The process of breaking down a conflict into smaller parts helps distance clients and make the exploration of their conflicts and disputes less overwhelming.

Briefly describing the route of this analysis at the beginning of the "N" stage, using Figure 4.2, is helpful for clients.

Some other points to consider about the intentions of this stage:

THE "N" STAGE IS A REAPPRAISAL OF THE "I" STAGE

In the "I" stage, coaches are likely to hear elements that clients will more fully explore in the "N" stage. However, what clients convey in the "I" stage is not the same as deconstructing their conflicts.

The "I" stage is the sort of information clients tell others. This is unlike the intention of the "N" stage, in which coaches methodically dig deeper in a way that distinguishes their role from the friends, family and colleagues with whom clients may have shared their conflict experience. Here, coaches help clients unpack the interaction and its dynamics for both people by systematically tracking and reflecting on how the situation evolved. This approach moves clients from the part of their brain where emotions prevail to the part where their analytical thinking takes over. Without the more comprehensive exploration that occurs in the "N" stage, the chances of clients gaining the awareness and insight that open up new thinking and possibilities are limited.

The "N" stage, then, with the analysis depicted in the (Not So) Merry-Go-Round of Conflict, is a type of cognitive reappraisal. It encourages clients to first, focus on and explore their own pattern when they were provoked by something the other person said or did. During this process, they gain insights and a better understanding of the elements of conflict they experienced. Next, a full examination of the sequence that the other person appeared to follow, based on the client's observations and experience of him or her, facilitates a different and more objective way of viewing the interaction. By using this methodical approach, clients "step outside" of themselves and view the situation through the other person's eyes. The increased self-awareness and the mutuality that emerges during this stage have the effect of neutralizing the conflict and the interpersonal dynamic.

SWITCHING ELEMENTS OF THE MERRY-GO-ROUND DOES NOT PRODUCE THE SAME LEVEL OF AWARENESS

The sequence depicted in Figure 4.2 facilitates a change in perspective when clients understand it as a common human pattern. For this reason, it is important to question clients in the order described. Switching the elements around in a non-sequential fashion does not facilitate the same insights into clients' conflict habits and patterns. Once clients gain an understanding of the sequence of the conflict pathway, they are able to use it to analyze future disputes.

IT TAKES TIME TO COACH CLIENTS THROUGH THIS STAGE

The "N" stage requires time for clients to process all the pertinent elements cognitively and emotionally. Asking clients to look at things through a new lens takes patience. Being silent, supportive and present while clients think and feel what is being asked of them in this exploration is crucial. Some clients may need an entire session to go through the conflict sequence, absorb new insights and be able to consider a different perspective.

> ### *Intention 2*
> To have the client identify and reflect on any new awareness, insights and perspectives, based on deconstructing the conflict/dispute

This part of the "N" stage has two considerations relating to the intention:

IDENTIFYING INSIGHTS HELPS SOLIDIFY THEM

Epiphanies gained in the "N" stage often have an impact on clients' choices about their goals and ways of reaching them. Later in the "R" stage, clients will construct or reconstruct their action plans by exploring different ways to manage their conflict, based in large part on insights gained from the (Not So) Merry-Go-Round of Conflict (Figure 4.2) in the "N" stage. It is therefore helpful for them to identify their insights and learning before moving on.

IF THERE ARE NO INSIGHTS, THAT TOO IS SIGNIFICANT

If clients say there is nothing different in the way they think and feel about themselves, the situation or the other person at the end of the "N" stage, it is important to consider why that is and not move on just yet. If nothing has changed for them, clients will proceed with the same mindset and heart-set they had when they began the process.

There are a variety of reasons why clients may not have shifted their feelings and perceptions. They may be experiencing a block or resistance that requires attention. Pride, denial, rage, shame and other emotions may prevail and preclude clients from stepping back from their conflict to analyze its elements. Clients who are introspective by nature and tend to intellectualize may have explored some of the elements of the conflict in their own way and reckon that they have already considered both perspectives. Others may not be open to or ready for self-examination, or may have some self-forgiveness or other self-care work to do. Some clients do not believe they contributed in any way to the dispute, so that considering both sides of the dynamic does not work for them.

Naming what coaches notice about clients when they say they haven't realized anything new from the "N" stage analysis often helps them to do some more and different exploration. For instance, if the coach senses a client's continuing anger, the coach could say something like, "I am still picking up some of the anger you talked about earlier."

This may help the client realize what he or she is conveying and encourage further exploration. Possible questions that may serve to open up the conversation are "What is still missing for you that you would like to understand about Michael (or this situation)?," "What were you hoping to figure out about the interaction that you haven't so far?" or "What may Michael not understand about you?" Approaches such as these often change the angle of the coaching conversation and assist clients to reconsider the situation, themselves and the other person. Occasionally, however, clients do not gain insights that shift their thinking and emotions until the "E" and "R" stages.

Intention 3

To have the client reassess the goal, having deconstructed the situation and gained different views

---

Breaking down their conflicts and considering both sides of the situation usually have an impact on clients' objectives. Therefore, before proceeding, coaches check out where the client is with respect to his or her goals.

At this point, clients may affirm their goal, giving them renewed resolve. Alternatively, increased understanding, clarity and insights gained in the "N" stage may lead them to change their goal. For instance, consider a scenario in which a client, Marta, comes to coaching with the goal of wanting to figure out what to say to her manager about a situation with a co-worker that is affecting their working relationship. In exploring the situation in the "N" stage, Marta realizes that she said some things that led to the co-worker's actions. That acknowledgment may lead her to decide instead that she would rather talk to the co-worker and see whether they are able to work things out together first.

Explore Choices

> ### *Intention 1*
> To help the client explore the possibilities for a plan of action to reach the stated goal

Having broken down the conflict/dispute by the end of the "N" stage of the CINERGY™ model, clients now begin to put things back together. The focus in the "E" stage is on the choices or options clients have to reach the goal they have now confirmed. The point that clients have choices about how to manage their conflicts and disputes is reinforced here.

Clients' choices may take a variety of forms. They may, for instance, want to list different ways to approach and manage their situation, or the range of workable solutions for the issues in dispute. If their objective is to communicate with the other person, the options to be analyzed may be a choice of method for connecting (email, phone, face to face). A client who has chosen a face-to-face meeting may want to consider options for the best location for that conversation. Any combination of these and other possibilities that they explore in this stage helps clients to formulate a plan of action, which is the intent of the first part of "E".

> ### *Intention 2*
> To help the client consider the risks and opportunities of the possible choices

Once clients identify their options for the action plan they are contemplating, the coach then helps them conduct a risk analysis of those choices. There are two main considerations here.

CLIENTS DO NOT HAVE ONLY ONE CHOICE AT THIS JUNCTURE

In brainstorming possibilities, clients may like several choices regarding a plan of action, whether it pertains to the issues, how to proceed or other matters. The client often needs to examine the range of options in depth before gaining clarity about which one(s) warrant further development. The coach facilitates this process by asking the client to look at the risks and opportunities of each choice.

Clients do not, however, have to commit to a single action at this juncture. Rather, many clients consider several choices within a context of how their plan may be envisioned or played out in the next stage ("R") before they are ready to determine which option has the highest potential for meeting their objective.

MUTUALITY CONTINUES AS A WORKING PREMISE

It is equally important in this stage for clients to consider, to the extent they are able, the pros and cons of their various choices from the other person's point of view. Doing so keeps mutuality at the center of decision-making and helps clients develop their plan of action based on more thorough and thoughtful analysis.

Even if clients determine that one or more of their choices may not be optimal from the other person's perspective, this does not necessarily preclude its selection. Under such circumstances, having considered the possible downsides, clients can still construct how they will move forward in the "R" stage.

Reconstruct the Situation

> ### Intention 1
> To have the client confirm a choice, or select the order of choices, to develop as a plan of action

The "R" stage is about helping clients optimize their potential plan in more specific ways. It focuses on helping them create the possibilities that are consistent with their goals and the choices they have just explored. At this time, coaches assist clients to construct or reconstruct their plan with their new insights and knowledge.

Construct involves designing a plan of action about an anticipated or previous conflict that they have not yet tried to address. *Reconstruct* occurs when clients want to revisit a situation that did not go well. Based on what they have learned in coaching, they plan how to manage themselves with the other person in an interaction that is different from the previous one.

Unless clients have selected a single course of action, the main question at this time is which choice to consider first of those identified in the "E" stage as possible ways forward.

Intention 2
To coach the client to create, reconstruct, rehearse and prepare option(s) for reaching the goal

---

This step involves (a) confirming the client's desired outcome of the choice selected, (b) setting up situations for the client to test and examine and (c) providing effective feedback and observations to the client, who practices new skills consistent with his or her goal and outcome.

Based on what clients unbundled in the "N" stage and the choices considered in the "E" stage, they now construct or reconstruct what it will take to make their action plan a reality. Clients start by working through their first (or only) choice. This means they consider the possible versions of what the plan will be, look and feel like. Coaches then facilitate clients' efforts to achieve their objective in a way that aligns with the desired outcome. If they have more choices, each follows the same process. The various aspects of this part of the "R" stage follow.

CONFIRMING THE CLIENT'S DESIRED OUTCOME
The desired outcome of clients' plan of action is the objective within their already identified goal. For instance, consider that a client's goal

in the "C" stage was to have a conversation with a co-worker about a dispute between them, and he or she has confirmed this at the end of the "N" stage. In the "R" stage, the question is: what does the client want as an outcome of the goal? Examples of outcomes may be to "clear the air," "make amends," "ensure we get on the same page about that matter," "be friends again," "agree to disagree" and so on.

By now, clients have had the opportunity to process their thoughts and feelings about their objectives, the situation and the other person. Having done so, they are better able to answer the question about their desired outcome. Concentrating on the client's intended result at this point is time well spent. The coach's task is to ensure that on-going coaching is consistent with what clients hope to achieve. The desired outcome is kept in the forefront as clients proceed to construct or reconstruct situations, conversations and other scenarios about how they intend to accomplish their goal with this result.

SETTING UP SITUATIONS FOR THE CLIENT TO TEST AND EXAMINE

The process of setting up clients' action steps in the "R" stage is pivotal to their success in carrying out their plans.

Preparation is necessary

This part of the "R" stage serves to focus clients on how their plan will become a reality. The more clients set their intentions and share the details of what it will look and feel like, including how they intend to be and be seen, the more aware and prepared they will be to proceed. If, for instance, clients want to reconstruct a conversation with the other person about a previous dispute, preparatory steps entail asking clients:

- To identify the key messages they wish to convey.
- To consider what the other person may want to convey in the interaction.
- To name what the other person may do or say that will be a trigger, and how they will respond this time.

- To identify what else they will do differently.
- To state what tone of voice, manner, body language and so on they intend to use that is consistent with the desired outcomes.
- To share their main concerns and the possible challenges for which they want to be most prepared.

Whether clients are preparing for a conversation or any other objective, gaining clarity about such preliminaries helps build a well-felt, well-thought-out foundation for envisioning, rehearsing, contemplating and ultimately accomplishing their goal and the desired outcome. Besides articulating their intentions, clients have the opportunity to reflect upon the skills they need to carry out their plan.

Rehearsing helps clients observe themselves and obtain input from coaches

If clients are open to doing so—and experience suggests that most are—practicing communication is an effective method for trying out different ways of interacting. Facilitating a rehearsal for clients serves many functions, not the least of which is to give them an opportunity to experience new ways of being, connecting, communicating and feeling. A rehearsal also allows the coach to offer clients specific and supportive feedback as to whether and how they are achieving both the form and substance of their plan of action. Repeated efforts build comfort and confidence as clients embed new and different ways of being in conflict. The more they practice, the easier the work becomes as clients realize they can rely on their own abilities and resources to achieve their objectives.

This stage does not necessarily entail a rehearsal per se. For instance, what if the client's goal is to change how she wants to be around the other person, such as "to remain cool and let my co-worker see I am not affected by his insults"? Coaches help clients examine how each of a series of possible situations will "look," how the client will feel, what he or she will be doing that is different and so on. In other words, coaches assist clients to "be" in the moments they are creating and to experience them sufficiently to be able to show up, respond and interact in the way they desire.

PROVIDING EFFECTIVE FEEDBACK AND OBSERVATIONS TO THE CLIENT

When clients are constructing or reconstructing their plans, the coach's role involves providing feedback and observations to assist them as they visualize, rehearse and experiment with their ideas and efforts. For instance, if the goal is to have a conversation, coaches listen and observe whether clients are being the way they want based on how they answered the coach's questions from the previous set-up part of this stage. The types of questions coaches ponder as they are listening during this process are:

- Is the client keeping his or her stated outcomes in the forefront?
- Is the client including all the messages he or she intends to convey?
- What is being expressed that is, and is not, in keeping with the client's intended tone of voice and manner?
- Is the client coming across the way he or she wants to come across, and making the intended changes?
- Is the client practicing the way he or she wants to receive and respond to the challenging messages expected from the other person?

It is important to obtain thorough criteria

In order to provide accurate observations and to help clients concentrate on accomplishing their goals, coaches ask them for detailed criteria so that their intentions are clear to themselves and to the coach. That is, it is most beneficial that clients articulate the specific ways they want to be in the construction or reconstruction of their actions. Their answers to questions about their tone of voice, body language and so on give coaches the requisite information for providing effective observations and feedback when clients proceed to rehearse, experiment, practice, envision and experience their anticipated scenarios.

For an example of obtaining thorough criteria, consider Jose, who says he want to be friendlier toward his co-worker when they discuss projects. The coach may ask Jose questions such as, "What will being friendlier sound and look like?," or "What will alert me to lack of friendliness in your voice, face or body?" In another example, if the client Kara is exploring how she intends to "look calm," the coach may say, "Please describe calm to me, Kara" or ask, "How will you know when you are losing your calmness?" and "How will I observe that?" These concrete ways of obtaining criteria facilitate effective feedback and the construction or reconstruction of the client's plans. (The skills of providing effective feedback and observations is discussed in greater detail in Chapter 5.)

Some further considerations about the intention of this part of the "R" stage follow.

What clients have learned is brought forward

In this step, coaches ask clients to identify what they know and have realized about the other person in coaching. For instance, insights that emerged in the "N" stage are brought into this step. Coaches also ask clients to reflect on what they learned that they will do differently based on new insights about themselves.

Similarly, the coach asks the client to contemplate previous experiences with the other person that may inform him or her how to proceed. Also, whatever clients have learned from conflict situations with others that may apply here may offer other considerations for their plan of action. Focusing their intentions, and being purposeful in these ways, optimizes clients' chances of success and gives them tools for future conflict and disputes.

Coaches "bring" the other person into the scenario or conversation

In the CINERGY™ model of coaching, coaches do not speak for or act as the other person in practice scenarios or conversations. Coaches and clients co-create the scene, with the clients enacting both themselves and the other person. In a rehearsal conversation, for instance, the client essentially conducts the dialogue as he or she contemplates the interaction between them. After every few sentences of a conversation or other exchange, the coach's role is to provide observations based on the criteria clients have previously articulated.

Clients may attempt each sentence or scenario several times until they are satisfied they are achieving their purpose before they move on to the next sentence or scenario. As clients go through this process, coaches also ask them to consider possible reactions from the other person for which they want to be prepared. Clients rehearse by trying out different ways of speaking, being, receiving anticipated messages and responding, until they gain the skills and confidence to proceed with their plan of action in ways that meet their intentions and desired outcome. This process often takes several sessions.

Coaches do not direct how clients communicate or interact

Coaches using this model do not provide suggestions—nor do they instruct or advise clients—on how to interact. Rather, the coach helps clients teach themselves by making the space for them to observe, experience and reflect on their actions and reactions as they practice and build their skills and abilities. In this way, clients self-discover how to accomplish what they set out to do in ways that are consistent with their goals.

Planning how, when and where the client's plan of action will unfold

At this stage, when applicable, clients or coaches may raise the matter of logistics. For example, a client who wants to initiate a challenging conversation with a colleague may not be sure of how to approach him or her to arrange that discussion. Sometimes however, logistics are raised in the "E" stage, especially if the client's plan poses concerns that require a risk analysis.

On the other hand, some clients do not want to figure out the related logistics until they have first constructed the interaction they aim to achieve, to see how it feels. In other cases, logistics may not arise until the "G" stage of the CINERGY™ model.

Ground the Challenges

> ### Intention
> To consider any challenges that may impede the client's plan, once it is confirmed

This step is about helping clients clear the way to make their goals a reality. It is distinguishable from the previous stage, in which clients address challenges within the context of the construction or reconstruction of their plan. The essence of the "G" stage is ensuring that clients have thought out anything that may preclude them from proceeding. Based on any stated challenges, coaches help clients work on how they will overcome them. The key to this stage is to keep clients positive, future-focused and able to move through the door they have already opened toward their goals.

Two further considerations about this intention follow.

SOME CHALLENGES HAVE BEEN PREVIOUSLY CONTEMPLATED

By this time, many clients have already discussed possible challenges that may impede their progress—for instance, when exploring the mutual risks and opportunities of their choices in the "E" stage, or while rehearsing and envisioning in the "R" stage. Clients who have not yet thought out any possible barriers to carrying out their objectives because they were not ready to (or for other reasons) will typically raise them at this time.

THE "G" STAGE DOES NOT APPLY UNTIL THERE IS A PLAN

The "G" stage applies only when clients have formulated a plan. The stage is not applicable if the session ends before they have figured out their way forward.

Yes, the Commitment

This last stage in the CINERGY™ model provides closure at the end of each session and serves as a stepping-off point for what happens next in coaching. This stage applies regardless of which part of the model has been reached at the time the session ends. The order of the following components of the "Y" stage is not important.

> ### *Intention 1*
> To confirm the client's next steps

Considerations about the intention of this part of the "Y" stage follow.

THIS COMPONENT IS ABOUT MOVING FORWARD

A question regarding next steps focuses clients on what they will do to progress further toward their objective before the next session. It is an optimistic question that invites clients to contemplate possibilities. Even if clients have not yet decided on their plan of action, a question such as, "What is your next step now?" is still suitable.

DOCUMENTING THE PLAN AND OTHER LEARNINGS FROM COACHING HELPS MANY CLIENTS

People who keep a journal, or take up journaling specifically during coaching, find it helpful to capture in writing their insights, thoughts, feelings and other self-discoveries they consider important. Even if they do not journal, some clients write down their next steps at this point in the "Y" stage. Then, when ready, they document a realistic timeframe for their action steps. Doing so establishes a degree of self-accountability and helps to ground clients and their plan. For many, it is also motivating to keep track of their coaching progress this way.

Intention 2

To hear the client's learnings ("takeaways")

The intention of this part of the "Y" stage is for clients to express what they learned or insights they gained in the session. In response to an inquiry about their takeaways, some clients reiterate insights that they may have discussed at earlier stages. Others elaborate on their overall experience of coaching so far, what they learned about themselves, or what parts of the process were particularly poignant or even disconcerting for them. If clients do not otherwise raise this latter topic, it is a good idea for the coach to check in with them from time to time to see how the coaching process is working for them.

Other considerations about the intention of this part of the "Y" stage follow.

CAPTURING INSIGHTS IS VITAL TO HOLDING ONTO THEM

Having clients focus on any new perspectives they have gained helps embed them. (See Chapter 1 regarding neuroscience findings on insights.) Because clients experience "aha's" at various times throughout coaching, it is meaningful for them to reflect back on these again at the end of the meeting. Some coaches provide a form for clients at the end of each session. A sample appears in Figure 4.3.

FIGURE 4.3 LOOKING FORWARD

To hold on to your awareness and learning in coaching, here are a few things to think about before we meet next:

1. The insights, discoveries, new and different thoughts and feelings that I gained in coaching today and that I want to consider further are:

_____

_____

_____

2. Some other things I want to reconsider from today's session that stood out for me are:

_____

_____

_____

3. In preparation for the next session, I plan to:

_____

_____

_____

Other comments:

_____

_____

_____

Thank you for considering your coaching experience and ways to make further progress.

CLIENTS' "TAKEAWAYS" HELP IN THE MEASUREMENT OF COACHING

Another important result when clients identify what they are taking away from their coaching experience is that they and the coach are able to determine the extent of clients' progress. If clients are not learning and gaining new awareness in the process, it is a signal for coaches to consider whether coaching is helping or if something else is going on for the client or between the client and the coach.

Similarly, when clients comment on their takeaways, their experience of the process, how they are feeling and so on, it is prudent for coaches to note any positive or negative impacts on their progress. Noticing any themes is important for continuing efforts to co-create the relationship and not to let unproductive aspects go without addressing them. This includes any areas that coaches may need to consider in their own role and how they are conducting the process. It is equally important to stay alert to the positive aspects that motivate, reassure and inspire clients.

> ### Intention 3
> To discuss a task for moving forward

Something that fosters ongoing reflection and builds the momentum of clients' coaching experience is an intentional and specific assignment of tasks—also called fieldwork—on which to focus their attention. A brief discussion on tasks between sessions appears in Chapter 3. Coaches usually alert potential clients to this aspect of the work in the early stages of client engagement. This topic, as it fits within the CINERGY™ model, is elaborated on here.

There are many reasons for clients to work on tasks between sessions:

- To prepare for the next session.
- To concretize next steps.
- To clarify or confirm aspects of the coaching journey so far.
- To continue to move forward on their goals.
- To keep insights and awareness in their consciousness.
- To take concentrated time to reflect on new learning.

Engaging clients in a discussion on what will help them progress typically happens at the end of each session. Documenting their tasks works well for many clients, and forwarding them to the coach on completion is a common practice.

COMPLETING TASKS IS ONE MEASURE OF ACCOUNTABILITY

Coaches are circumspect about attributing lack of commitment or accountability to clients who do not work on a task between sessions. Many variables factor into whether clients do a task or tasks. Ideas that seem appropriate at the close of a session may not resonate in the days that follow. For instance, the client may begin contemplating a different goal. Or, the seeds that were planted in a session may generate new thoughts and feelings that make the identified task irrelevant. These and other reasons may get in the way of clients' doing the task(s) discussed, or even considering alternatives. However, if a client repeatedly does not do the discussed tasks between sessions, a conversation is warranted to ensure that coaches stay aware of what may be happening in this regard.

TASKS MAY BE CLIENT- OR COACH-INSPIRED

Client-inspired tasks

Finding out what clients want to work on before the next coaching session helps them own the task and focus their energy. A range of ideas commonly unfolds. For instance, some people identify what parts of the model intrigued, concerned or surprised them and choose to revisit these to reflect further on them. Clients may select tasks related to obtaining relevant information and resources to help them reach their goals. Other clients choose to try out a new skill with a friend or colleague, or practice a conversation in front of a mirror. The possibilities are limitless.

Coach-inspired tasks

Coach-inspired tasks are often different from clients' ideas. Coaches remain aware of clients' progress and typically stretch them to take on and consider aspects of their coaching journey they may not themselves contemplate.

Tasks that coaches commonly suggest also relate to whichever stage of the model the session is in when it is ending. For instance, if the session ends just as the "E" stage is about to begin, the coach may explain that in the next stage, the client will have the opportunity to explore possible options for reaching his or her goal and the risks and opportunities of each possibility. Inviting the client to consider these in advance is one possible task related to this stage.

CRITERIA FOR COACH-INSPIRED TASKS

When proposing a task, coaches may consider the following criteria:

- *Specific.* Concrete tasks generally work best. For example, consider Thomas, who will be going into the "R" stage and whose goal is to have a difficult conversation with his manager. Rather than a vague suggestion, such as, "You may want to think about what you could say in that conversation," a more specific task helps provide more focus for Thomas. This may sound like, "Since the next stage is on preparing for that conversation with your manager, here are a number of things you may want to consider for our next session. What messages do you want to convey? How do you want to be perceived? And what are you most concerned about?"

- *Pertinent.* Coach-inspired tasks also tune into clients' insights, reactions, concerns or challenges experienced in their sessions. The coaching process may give rise, also, to doubts, emotional reactions and so on that can potentially prevent clients from moving forward. In some cases, coaches may suggest tasks that ask clients to reconsider such areas before the next session. (Some clients may zero in on these areas themselves.) As well, because coaches usually see and hear things of which clients are not always aware, they are in an ideal position to suggest tasks pertaining to their observations of clients' efforts. For instance, if in the "R" stage the client, Aida, found it challenging to consider what she wants to achieve in her conversation with her co-worker Peter, one possible task might be, "May I suggest that you consider, between now and our next meeting, how you want to feel at the end of your conversation with Peter?" and, "What do you want your relationship with Peter to be?"

- *Relevant.* Because one way that progress in coaching is measured is whether clients are reaching their identified objectives, it is important for coaches to ensure that any suggested tasks are relevant to their goal and move them forward. (Needless to say, the coach will wish to explore any factors that preclude clients' progress, such as those just discussed.)

- *Different*. A way of stretching clients is to encourage them to continue to consider a different and more positive way of looking at themselves, the situation, the other person or some combination of these. A related task helps clients reframe their situation. Questions for clients to consider as fieldwork might be: "What in this situation now gives you a sense of optimism?," "What possibilities exist for you now that didn't when we started?," "What will be different for you when you reach your goal?" or "What do you need to be able to experience a sense of accomplishment about this matter that you do not yet have?" The notion of suggesting that clients consider something different may also take the form of asking them to stand back and observe what is happening for themselves, for example: "If someone you care about were watching you, what would they notice that is different about you since you began working through this conflict?"

Intention 4

To acknowledge the client's efforts and end on a positive note

---

Acknowledging clients is something coaches do throughout coaching sessions to support, validate, motivate and inspire their progress. (Chapter 5 elaborates on this skill.) Acknowledging clients at the end of each session is emphasized here.

As sessions wind down, clients typically experience a range of emotions and thoughts. Many clients who engage in conflict management coaching report that they feel relieved that the related stress starts to abate and hopeful about finding their way through the situation. Feeling inspired, fatigued, supported, energized and a combination of these and other responses about their coaching experience is also common for clients at this time. Other clients feel unabating anxiety and concern about their situation, or other emotions that are pessimistic in nature. In any case, the coach's acknowledgment and appreciation of the client's feelings and progress are particularly meaningful for clients as they contemplate where they have been and where they are going in their coaching journey. The importance of ending each coaching session on a reassuring, positive, supportive and optimistic note cannot be overstated.

SUMMARY

- The CINERGY™ model provides a mental compass that helps both coaches and clients focus on clients' conflict management goals. Each of the seven stages has specific intentions, and knowing what these are facilitates coaches' use of the framework to assist clients in reaching their objectives.

- In the development of the CINERGY™ model, study group members (and many clients since that time) gained most when each stage was explored methodically and thoroughly, step by step. If clients wander in their journey of self-discovery, coaches use their instincts and training to help them explore the "side roads." Coaches then refocus clients on the map of the model so that they can move forward and accomplish their conflict management goals when they are ready to do so.

- This model of conflict management coaching helps clients reflect on themselves, their situation and the other person through a relational, cognitive, emotional and behavioral lens of analyzing conflict. Gaining increased awareness about what happened for them and the other person through the use of the (Not So) Merry-Go-Round of Conflict helps clients reappraise their perspective. In this process, clients re-script their situation and gain insights into themselves and the other person. This analysis and the incremental nature of the model ultimately stretch clients to shift their usual style of interacting and responding and to find alternative ways of being in conflict. Clients also gain new awareness that may be applied to future conflicts and disputes.

- Coaches are the navigators for their clients' journey. Although the coach holds the map, it is up to clients to make their own discoveries and choose the optimal way forward that meets their needs and desired outcomes.

Note

1. Robert Bolton and Dorothy Grover Bolton, *People Styles at Work: Making Bad Relationships Good and Good Relationships Better* (New York: Amacom, 1996), 9.

Conflict Management Coaching Skills

There are many skills that coaches, mediators, HR professionals, leaders and others have honed from current and previous training, educational backgrounds and experience. This chapter includes a number of such competencies and suggests additional considerations for coaching individuals to engage in conflict effectively. Because being skillful as coaches also entails conducting themselves ethically, this chapter proposes model Standards of Ethical Conduct for conflict management coaches. The standards are pertinent to the CINERGY™ coaching model, though most terms are broadly applicable. They provide a framework for discussing ethics for this specialty, while recognizing that there is not a regulatory coaching entity at this time.

The Coach's Skill Set

A mutually respectful and synergistic coach–client relationship is undoubtedly an essential foundation for working together. Establishing that relationship requires the coach to bring into play a variety of specific skills that are discussed in this chapter.

Developing the Coaching Relationship

People who choose to become coaches typically have innate qualities that include strong intuition, thoughtfulness, empathy and compassion. Building rapport with clients requires these and many other characteristics, including flexibility and a willingness and openness to understand clients' perspectives, to be honest, to convey respect, to remain nonjudgmental and to be optimistic with and for them. Such traits not only help clients to connect with the coach. They also facilitate clients' learning and growth and their comfort with the coaching process and themselves within it.

The groundwork for developing this relationship begins in the inquiry stage and is concretized when the contract to work together is confirmed. The thrust of developing and co-creating the coaching relationship is that coaches are collaborators and partners with clients in their efforts to reach their conflict management objectives. To be able to stretch clients and challenge them to step up and be accountable, the coach's role, among other things, requires creating a milieu in which clients will thrive and progress. Coaches want their clients to succeed, and to facilitate success, they seek to discover what each client requires. It is also necessary for coaches to be clear on what is expected from clients, including their commitment to do the work.

Commonly, clients who seek or are referred to coaching know little, if anything, about the process or the coach. They bring with them varying levels of adaptability, uncertainty, fear, and states of mind and heart as a result of their situation. All these have an impact on how clients connect with the coach.

Moreover, some people arrive with various notions about coaching; others do not know what to expect. Even if clients have been coached in the past, their current experience may be quite different owing to the new coach's style, manner, personality and the objectives they now want to accomplish. Though some clients who are referred to conflict management coaching may demonstrate resentment and resistance, others will approach coaching as the opportunity it is meant to be and embrace the process showing enthusiasm, curiosity and eagerness to participate. Along this spectrum is a range of responses to coaching and to the coach, some of which may present challenges. In any case, time spent on developing a solid alliance builds a foundation for the work to be done.

Inextricably intertwined with strengthening rapport and connection is the importance of establishing trust. Trust refers to the confidence that clients have in the coach's integrity, expertise and professionalism. Complicating the development of trust for the client are variables to do with personal or professional histories where trust has been challenged, how the client came to coaching, his or her degree of vulnerability, how the coach was selected, suspicions relating to the level of confidentiality, lack of clarity about the client's role, the coach's role or the process and so on. Throughout coaching, conflict management coaches remain alert as to whether the coach–client relationship is intact and strengthening. If signs appear that indicate otherwise, it is incumbent on coaches to raise any related concerns with clients.

There are many ways that coaches co-create the relationship and make efforts to develop and sustain trust. The following are some proven ways for coaches to connect:

- Getting to know each client as a person, not just as a person in conflict.
- Being transparent from the beginning about the terms of confidentiality, the process, the methods used, the respective roles and so on.
- Being punctual and prepared.

- Acknowledging and understanding clients' emotions.
- Refraining from overtalking or personalizing.
- Assuring clients that the coach is there to support them to reach their goals.
- Inviting clients to provide their feedback on the coach and the process, and welcoming their input.
- Sharing honest observations and feedback, and checking in about how the input is being received.
- Acknowledging clients' insights, progress, new actions and constructive changes, and appreciating their efforts.
- Demonstrating respect for and understanding of clients' perspectives, needs, expectations, hopes and concerns.
- Demonstrating authenticity, consistency, reliability, integrity and professionalism.
- Managing the coaching process with confidence and care.
- Walking beside clients rather than leading them to where the coach thinks they ought to go.
- Collaborating on accountability measures and fieldwork/tasks and following through on the related responsibility of monitoring clients' progress.
- Adhering to the principle of self-determination.
- Modeling effective communication.

Another recommended way that helps co-create the relationship is for coaches to ask clients to share their style of learning and of communicating, and to honor this information as the process unfolds. It often assists, too, when coaches gain an understanding of the influences that inform clients' ways of interacting in conflict.

One other important aspect of connecting requires coaches to reflect on, observe and address not only how clients are relating to the coach throughout the process, but how the coach is relating to clients. This includes being aware of comfort levels with clients' issues, personalities and other variables that present potential challenges. It is common for coaches to work with a supervisor or peer group, or obtain coaching themselves, about any related concerns. Whenever the interrelationship dynamics are not working for the client or coach, it is time to assess whether the fit is suitable.

Being Present

Being present means that coaches stay aware and in the moment as clients move through the model and their process of self-discovery. It is about extending energy to be fully "there" for them. Being present also requires coaches to be centered and focused before going into a session so that they can give the client their full attention. It is about being prepared to hold, accept and receive the client's heart and mind, in understanding and attuned ways.

Coaches often work with clients to ensure that they, too, are ready and able to concentrate on the coaching process. To do so requires clients to have a mindset and heart-set that is flexible and open to create, to reflect, to think out possibilities, to get in touch with their inner resources and potential and to make important decisions about their lives. When clients come to a session or call and appear or admit to being distracted (or if this becomes evident during the conversation), many coaches find it helpful to spend some time assisting them to focus so that they are fully present. Clients may already have methods they use; otherwise, coaches may suggest meditation, breathing exercises or other mindfulness methods for those who are amenable to learning tools of this nature (which they may also incorporate into other aspects of their lives).

Managing the Process

The CINERGY™ model provides a framework within which clients methodically and incrementally progress toward their goals. In their anxiety to attain these, clients may want to jump ahead before gaining sufficient understanding of their conflict, including their contribution to it. This behavior may be the way they usually function when in conflict and may even have played a part in their current situation.

Being transparent about the stages of the coaching model and managing it requires coaches to trust the map that the framework provides. Besides adhering to the stages of the model, its premises and intentions, managing the process also means that coaches stay patient with the client and themselves as they progress together toward the client's objectives. A client's long-term incompatibilities, entrenched habits, strong emotions, anxiety to solve things quickly and other variables that reflect previous challenges with conflict are not quickly fixed. Coaches know that the same heart and mind that embroil clients in their conflicts are not the same heart and mind that will help them reconstruct more effective ways of being in conflict.

One important part of the CINERGY™ model, and a skill in managing this particular process, is to refrain from providing advice or opinions. Coaches operate on the basis that clients are the authority on themselves and are creative, resourceful and able to decide and act on a course of action for reaching their goals without being told how to do so. Suggesting ways to "fix" situations, or providing opinions about what may work for clients, comes from good intentions. However, solving clients' problems for them interferes with their efforts and does not enable them to rely on their own resources, abilities and creativity. Also, advice-giving and offering opinions are typically focused on the outcome the giver has in mind. That is, the genesis of advice is the giver's rule book, beliefs, values, judgments, assumptions and possibly, desires about what would be a good result. Such advice is often what coaches would tell themselves to do or say in similar circumstances.

The skill of managing the process, then, requires letting go of any tendencies to take on the responsibility of shaping an outcome and leading clients to what coaches think is best for them. As one CINERGY™ workshop participant said, "This model is about helping clients realize that they already know how to fish."*

---

* A reference to the proverb by Lao Tsu, "Give me a fish, I have food for a day. Teach me how to fish, and I will have food for every day."

Further, providing their own perspectives precludes coaches from using other, more appropriate coaching tools for helping clients explore their own potential, motivations, ideas, concerns and ways of proceeding that fit within their personal, professional, cultural and other contexts.

Intentional Hearing

It is not possible to discuss coaching skills without including listening as a core competency. Listening may consist of reflecting back, acknowledging, summarizing, paraphrasing, restating, validating emotions, reframing, noting facial and body language and using silence. Coaches, mediators and others in the human services typically use these methods judiciously, strategically and thoughtfully.

Intentional hearing is a skill that requires coaches to be deliberate about what each client needs to feel heard. This part of the chapter discusses how coaches can accomplish the proficiency of intentional hearing and how they may observe whether clients perceive they are being heard.

A starting point is to ask clients, when coaching begins, how they know when others are listening and hearing them. Similarly, there is wisdom in confirming with clients from time to time whether they feel heard and if not, what may work better for them. This type of inquiry models openness and flexibility, and most people are able to share what they need if they experience they are not being heard. Coaching conversations of this nature are another way to share the responsibility of the coaching process and to work collaboratively.

The suggested components of intentional hearing are contained in the acronym CHOICES: Concentrate, Hear, Observe, Invite, Clarify, Engage and Silent listening.

oncentrate

> Concentrate unequivocally on the client, free
> of distractions, including the coach's agenda.

This component reminds coaches to leave their assumptions, hopes,
expectations and ego out of the sessions. Rather than being preoccupied with their own thoughts and views, coaches focus on their clients,
their objectives and needs. They do not complete clients' thoughts or
assume that they understand what they are saying. This is one way of
being present for clients and being attuned to them and their coaching
journey. Concentrating unequivocally also means being intentional—
that nothing extraneous will distract or interrupt the coach or client.

Coaches' concentration is evident when they see that clients remain present and focused on the process and their objectives. Clients
become increasingly relaxed, share openly and easily and do not show
signs of losing their attentiveness.

H ear

> Hear what is being said, what is not being said, what
> emotions are evident, what is dissonant.

What coaches hear and do not hear are major elements of intentional
hearing. Coaches listen for clients' emotions, hopes, choices, possibilities, resistance, expectations, needs, level of commitment, worries,
values, goals, growing or diminishing trust and so on. Coaches hear
speech patterns, ambiguities, ambivalences, changes in clients' tone of
voice, their choice of words, their rate of speech, the use of metaphors
and repeated or emphasized comments. Similarly, intentional hearing
means coaches notice dissonance, gaps and other signs that don't seem

to align with the messages clients are conveying. Coaches also hear underlying thoughts and feelings and consider such things as "Is that contrary to what she just said?," "Am I hearing the sound of fear in his voice?" or "How is what she is saying relevant to her goal?"

Clients experience this aspect of intentional hearing by expressing surprise when coaches point out things that they themselves are not hearing or conscious of. In response, many gain insights and explore more deeply what they are saying and feeling. Others start to hear themselves differently and pay closer attention to what they are thinking and experiencing. As one client once remarked: "I just heard myself repeat that she *disarms* me about the way she acts. Disarm is really a war word! Wow! I do feel like we're at war and that she's got the weapons and I don't. I never thought of it that way." This type of client-generated reflection (and metaphor) that emanates from even just one word noted by coaches or clients helps clients dig deeper and gain important insights.

O bserve

> Observe clients' body language, including facial expressions, demeanor, movement, reactions.

Attitudes, facial expressions, gestures and body language speak volumes. Using the well-known listening technique of observation, coaches perceive things that clients are not always able to see about their own bodies, faces and ways of presenting themselves. Coaches also identify any lack of connection between clients' body or facial language and their expressed emotions. By sharing observations and engaging clients in a conversation about such details, coaches are able to hold up the mirror for clients to reflect upon themselves. An example might be, "I just heard you say you are feeling better about the situation. At the same time, I observed you were clenching your fists and your facial expression looked to be sad."

Here again, clients are often surprised at what coaches see. They gain insights and increased awareness when they hear such observations. Clients also experience this aspect of listening by becoming more conscious of their body language and noting inconsistencies between their verbal and non-verbal messages. Some clients may share comments about somatic habits that others have remarked on, such as fidgeting, tightening their jaw, smiling or laughing when they are nervous and so on. Other clients may become more attuned to and comment on what they observe about the other person's body language or demeanor.

Invite

> Invite clients to use and develop their intuition based on what coaches hear and observe.

This aspect of intentional hearing relates to what coaches sense and intuit about clients and their words, feelings, disposition and so on. Some coaches have stronger instincts than others, and some rely on them more than others. In either case, it is important that coaches acknowledge that their intuition is not always compatible with the way things actually are for clients. With this in mind, inviting clients to express their intuition empowers them to get in touch with and to use their own instincts. An example of such an invitation may be simply, "What are your gut instincts telling you right now?," "What's your inner dialogue about that?" or "I'm curious to know what your intuition is telling you about what she said."

When clients experience this aspect of intentional hearing, they gain comfort and confidence to consider and explore their intuition and the content of their internal discussions. They increasingly share whatever is on their mind and in their heart that they may previously have censored or suppressed. Coaches may hear statements like,

"Something I've been wondering about for a while is …" or "This is the first time I have actually said this out loud." Clients may also look surprised or relieved, and express other responses, when they discover the ease of tapping into their insights. As one client remarked, "I feel as though I am being given permission to think for myself."

larify

> Clarify only when necessary.

Many practitioners use summarizing, paraphrasing and reframing as a way of clarifying what clients say and demonstrating that they are listening, and these are acknowledged coaching proficiencies. However, it is not always necessary to use these techniques, or to use them extensively.

"Clarify only when necessary" means limiting the tendency to summarize what coaches perceive clients are saying. The coach may do this especially when the client's words are unclear or confusing, but such inferences may be incorrect. Leaving it to clients to provide their own interpretations empowers them to think things out more and articulate what they are experiencing in their own words.

At these times, straightforward invitations work well, such as, "Please clarify what you said at that time," "Tell me more about that" or "The part about when John was late again isn't clear." Also, "Please explain that again" or "I didn't quite get what happened at that point" accomplish this.

Clients experience this aspect of intentional hearing by getting clearer and more certain about what they are saying. They reflect longer and find more words to express their experiences and feelings.

Despite the caution about overusing skills such as summarizing and reframing, the skill of paraphrasing, particularly, has several important uses; when it is not overly used, it can heighten a client's sense of being heard. For instance, paraphrasing serves to "bottom-line" extensive information and is especially meaningful if the brief summary contains the client's own words. Paraphrasing is also useful when coaches think they missed something and want to ensure they clearly grasp the client's meaning and statements.

ngage

> Engage clients in a dialogue about what coaches sense.

How coaches express their hunches, instincts and concerns about what they observe when clients communicate their experiences and their related emotions is a skill in and of itself. The idea of this aspect of intentional hearing is best demonstrated when coaches do not jump to conclusions, but rather name the observation and at the same time, remain unattached to what is sensed and expressed. Coaches consider that clients possibly do not want to make the coach appear "wrong," and may defer to their perspective even though it may not accurately reflect what is going on for them.

Coaches accept that even when they make an observation that appears to resonate for clients, there may be more to it—the client may be experiencing something else. To have this discussion effectively, coaches remain open to other possibilities than those they intuit and express. Rather, they convey what they are picking up in a curious, open and flexible way that engages clients to challenge coaches' instinctive views and tap into their own. For example, coaches may preface their observations with, "I could be wrong here ..." or "Something struck me about your statement just now ... What's your take on that?"

Clients experience this aspect of intentional hearing when they appear confident that coaches view them as the expert on their own thoughts, feelings, actions, decisions and so on. They may respond to hunches with a rush of insight, with agreement or with a push back. When coaches raise intuitive thoughts in an open way, clients are comfortable disagreeing with what is said and conveying what is on their mind and in their heart. Here, as with other aspects of intentional hearing, they may express thoughts and feelings they have not yet discussed about their conflicts, themselves or the other person.

S ilent Listening

> Silent listening facilitates hearing.

Providing silent support is a crucial part of the skill of intentional hearing. In the CINERGY™ model, as in many other coaching frameworks, the notion that "less is more" prevails when it comes to the amount that coaches talk. Being silent means not completing clients' thoughts or distracting them with a voice other than their own. It means not synthesizing and reframing clients' answers with the coach's interpretations.

Silence is often more powerful than saying or doing anything except nodding and otherwise showing, by body language, that the coach is listening and hearing. Being silent at these times facilitates clients' abilities to explore different ways of thinking and feeling. It demonstrates trust in clients that, with time and quiet contemplation, they will find and express their own words to describe and reframe their experiences of conflict.

When clients feel listened to through this aspect of intentional hearing, they respond by reflecting more and talking more. They ultimately become more focused on what they say and appear to feel increasingly safer to share as they process their new insights. Many clients report a sense of liberation with their thoughts, imaginations and feelings. They express themselves more freely and openly, and are energized by the experience of being heard.

With regard to this reference to a sense of freedom, coaches who employ the elements of CHOICES share that they, too, experience a liberating effect. They report letting go of tendencies to interpret, reframe, search for issues to identify and summarize. They talk less and refrain from doing the client's work and problem-solving. Coaches who are masterful at intentional hearing also listen closely to themselves and what they are feeling, thinking and experiencing during the course of coaching. If they begin to judge and lead, if they lose their attention or if they let their egos, needs and assumptions prevail, the signs of doing so are likely to show on their face, in their body language and in their voice and words, adversely influencing the client's journey, their relationship and the process. The skill of listening to themselves requires that coaches remain aware of the ways in which they stray from the purpose of intentional hearing and undertake the requisite work to rectify any tendencies in this regard.

Possibility Questioning

Framing questions in ways that evoke awareness, that challenge in supportive ways, that motivate action and that stretch clients to move forward is one of the most powerful and transformational tools that coaches learn and use. Through effective and meaningful questions, clients experience epiphanies—those moments when they have new and different insights, ideas, thoughts or feelings. Questions that are powerful also inspire, facilitate creativity, clarify and plant seeds for later discovery.

Possibility questions invite clients to reflect on and reappraise their perspectives, so that they consider alternative viewpoints. They help clients shift their way of thinking and feeling about their situation and the other person. These types of questions ask clients to tap into their inner thoughts and emotions, some of which they are not consciously aware. Possibility questions are future-oriented, solution-focused and optimistic and, as in the appreciative inquiry approach, are framed in a way that replaces deficit judgment with openness to the positive.[1]

A few examples of possibility questions:

- What do you suppose this experience is meant to teach you?
- What will help you be who you want to be in that conversation?

- How will it be for you when you reach your goal?
- What other approach aligns with what you hope to achieve?
- How will you be different the next time so that you stay true to the outcome you want?
- What doesn't she know about you that may help improve things between you?
- What don't you know about her that may help you move forward?
- How do you want to be perceived in your future interactions with him?
- How will you know that you are achieving that objective?
- Imagine that you had all the skills you need to manage that situation. What will you be doing and saying?
- When you succeeded in managing a conflict well in the past, what did you do then that might also work here?

Possibility questions may also be "two-footed."[2] Such questions engage different parts of the brain and ask people to keep their outcomes in the forefront. For instance, a two-footed version of a question such as, "What is something you want to be sure to say to Sally?" might be, "What is something Sally may want to hear from you that is in keeping with your goal to make amends?" In this example, one foot relates to the content of the message considering what Sally may want to hear. The second foot relates to what the client is aiming to achieve for himself or herself.

One "intentional hearing" skill connected to possibility questioning is the skill of being silent. Being quiet after asking these types of questions is especially important, as silence respects the various ways that clients process new queries and the accompanying thoughts and emotions they inspire. Silence opens up space for clients to let their thoughts wander. Exercising patience goes along with this skill, especially with clients who are anxious about their conflicts. Coaches' patience also reduces pressure on those who may otherwise respond in haste and make decisions without reflection.

Empathizing with Clients

Empathizing is mentioned here as a skill to emphasize the importance of helping clients who need and want to express the emotional impact of their conflicts. As discussed in Chapter 2, emotions are inevitably present when people engage in conflicts and disputes, and have an impact on problem-solving, creativity and decision-making. Ensuring that clients know their coach hears and empathizes with them facilitates their comfort to express this dimension of conflict and the words that reflect what they are experiencing. Again, allowing clients the space and pace to voice what is important to them, and the impact of their conflicts, is integral to their progress. However, as also discussed, not all clients want to talk at length about their emotions.

The coach needs to know how and when to transition clients who do share their feelings away from what upset them so that they can focus on their goals and the future direction of coaching. (Chapter 4 discusses this delicate balance in the context of the "I" stage of the model.) To accomplish this transition and facilitate clients' movement forward requires that coaches demonstrate confidence in working with a range of emotions without becoming overwhelmed or enmeshed in clients' feelings. This sometimes occurs when coaches' personal and professional foundations are not solid, or their own experiences pull them into clients' emotions.

Extending empathy to themselves is crucial for coaches doing conflict-related work. This means recognizing when they are not in the frame of mind and heart to give their best, and knowing when they require assistance to strengthen their own capacities. Clients privilege coaches when they share themselves in the ways that coaching invites. To return the honor that comes with being trusted in this way, it is critical that coaches stay alert to internal signals and take care of themselves. It is also necessary that they identify and work on what they need to stay grounded, to maintain their focus and integrity and their ability to feel and demonstrate genuine empathy for their clients. The topic of self-work is relevant here again and discussed later in this chapter.

Providing Observations

Clients who seek or are referred to conflict management coaching commonly demonstrate behaviors that do not work for them. These may include their body language, facial gestures, tone of voice, demeanor, temper, attitude, way of expressing themselves and so on. Even if clients are aware that their ways of interacting are problematic, they may not know just how they are perceived or the impact they have on others.

Giving specific feedback and observations is an integral part of coaching. This requires coaches to remain cognizant of how they convey their input and how clients receive it. As with the "Observe" component of intentional hearing, which this section elaborates on, what coaches notice that clients cannot is crucial for enabling them to gain increased awareness about their conflict conduct. This is one way that coaches provide clients the opportunity to stand back and look at themselves and ultimately learn alternative, more effective ways of being in conflict.

Observations may be conveyed in various ways, such as through coaches' possibility questions that evoke clients' self-reflection. An example might be, "What did you notice about yourself when you just told me about how enraged you are with Joe?" Direct statements are also helpful, such as, "I just heard your voice go up and noticed that your hands began to tap on the table when you talked about Joe."

Even with telephone coaching, coaches are able to tune into cues and work with clients to identify their body language, tone of voice and so on. Engaging clients to observe themselves and monitor their own facial and body language is a powerful technique. It engenders self-reflection that effectively helps clients increase their awareness and gain insights. Sometimes literally using a mirror facilitates this process.

How clients receive coaches' observations depends on numerous factors, including how they historically hear anything that may be construed as criticism, the degree of trust and rapport between the coach and client and the client's general readiness to accept feedback. Many clients are eager to receive input and expect it from the coach.

Others come to coaching with a range of emotions about their situation and the other person in their conflict that affect how they hear and receive feedback.

Clients who are referred to coaching and who perceive it as an involuntary intervention sometimes experience heightened reactions to a coach's feedback. They may feel that it undermines their identity as an adult, a leader, a hard worker and so on. Coaches remain vigilant about signs of related distress. David Rock states that if clients have "an unconscious expectation that equates feedback to criticism, they may perceive this as a threat" to their status, that is, "not looking good in the eyes of someone important."[3] This reaction relates to perceived threats that may lead to reduced functioning of the prefrontal cortex (see Chapter 2, "Emotions in Conflict"). Rock goes on to recommend asking permission (another coaching skill, to be discussed next) and using an appreciative perspective that primes clients to receive feedback constructively.

Because some clients will respond adversely to comments about how they conduct themselves and interact, it is helpful for coaches to explain, when coaching begins, that offering feedback is part of their role and to ask clients how they best receive such input. It is also important, of course, to have first developed a trusting and supportive relationship for clients to be able to hear and accept observations in the intended spirit of the coach and coaching.

Feedback and observations can be delivered in different ways, and coaches' various styles and relationship with the client determine their manner and its effect. Coaches learn how to provide observations in ways that are helpful, thoughtful and encouraging. Meaningful observations are balanced, clear, respectful and understandable. Effective delivery of input may be referred to as the CSI of feedback—Concrete, Supportive and Inspiring.

Any negative responses to coaches' efforts to give feedback provide opportunities to coach clients about how they receive input. This is also a chance for coaches to consider how they are conveying feedback and whether there is work to be done in this regard. The primary goal, in any case, is that clients hear and understand what the coach is saying, that it is relevant to what they are aiming to achieve and that they find it useful and supportive.

Here is one example of a real-life situation and some different ways for the coach to provide observations:

One of the things Ryan was working on in coaching was a series of complaints about his apparent tendency to be "abrupt" with his staff. Many perceive that he puts them down with this mannerism, and there have been a number of disputes with his staff in this regard.

Ryan's goal is to understand what factors lead to his abrupt responses and to better manage his reactions when he is provoked. He has previously told the coach what he thinks "abrupt" means based on feedback he has received from his boss, which reflects the complaints of his direct reports. In a coaching session a few weeks later, and after beginning to examine what leads to his reactions, Ryan was abrupt with the coach's attempts to explore his tendency to be abrupt, saying, "There's nothing more to talk about here."

A coach's input might be, "When you said, 'there's nothing to talk about,' your reaction fit your definition of abrupt. Here's a chance to explore what was going on. May I share the impact?" Or, "What did I just say that you reacted abruptly to?" Another coach might simply ask, "What just happened there?" Or, "Ryan, may I share some thoughts that just came up for me?" With affirmation, the coach might say something like, "I seem to have struck a chord just now when you reacted to my attempt to explore your tendency to be abrupt, by being abrupt."

Whether coaches employ examples of this nature or other responses that reflect different styles, engaging the client in a non-judgmental and non-defensive way is necessary for keeping the dialogue positive and productive. In this case, there is a direct opportunity to coach Ryan further about what is behind his reaction, how it works and does not work for him and his staff and other such aspects that help him examine what leads to abruptness and how to better manage his response.

Developmental opportunities commonly arise within coaching sessions where clients demonstrate the very behaviors they are working on. Though there are other times too within the CINERGY™ model when coaches share their observations, the "R" stage is frequently a time when clients practice the different ways they want to be, or say things as part of their plan of action.

Coaches rely on clients to provide the criteria for assessing their attempts to interact in different ways and conduct themselves according to their desired outcomes. The coach's role is then to point out behaviors that are counterproductive and inconsistent with the client's stated goal. By providing constructive and supportive observations, the coach invites clients to notice themselves and explore ways of adjusting their mannerisms, behaviors and demeanor in keeping with their objectives.

Requesting Permission

One example of giving feedback in the previous scenario started with the coach asking Ryan for permission before proceeding to do so. This is one of the many ways coaches remain respectful of clients' sensibilities with regard to receiving feedback by asking for permission first, rather than assuming the input is welcome at the time. When asked, clients may say "no," which lets the coach know that there is reluctance to receiving feedback.

If that happens, it may be a signal about how clients are experiencing the process and the coach's observations. Or, the client may not yet be ready or able to take in feedback. It is crucial for coaches to discuss any resistance at the time and remain conscious about how they deliver their comments.

Here are some suggested ways of requesting permission to provide input in a non-threatening manner:

- "May I share something I just heard?"
- "Is this a good time for me to tell you what I observed?"
- "Would you like to hear my thoughts on that?"
- "I am wondering if some of my input may be helpful here. May I?"
- "This is one of those times I mentioned where I offer my observations. Does that work for you right now?"

Using Metaphors

There are many creative ways that coaches help clients examine their conflicts and disputes and one way is through the use of metaphors. Metaphors are comparisons that help summarize or explain an event or person. By using metaphors, many people are able to "create a mental map quickly and with minimal effort."[4] Metaphors can also help clients who are challenged in their efforts to envision an action, to uncover values and to identify blocks to get through an impasse. It is common for coaches to use, and to hear clients use, metaphors as a way of expressing themselves and their circumstances.

A few examples of metaphors: "He acted like a caged animal," "She was higher than a kite until he came into the room," "Talking to him is like talking to a wall" and "There is an elephant in the room." By eliciting or developing visual images that may effectively describe their experiences in different ways, clients view their situation differently.

Whatever the metaphor symbolizes for clients is often rich with specific meaning for them. By exploring the metaphor in the coaching conversation, coaches enable clients to make more connections. Experience suggests that before using clients' metaphors as part of the dialogue and line of inquiry in the coaching model, it works well to encourage the client, first, to discuss its meaning and clarify how it applies in that moment.

As another example, consider the client, Pablo, who describes an impasse in his relationship with his co-worker. Pablo says, "There's a big wall between us since our argument and it won't crumble no matter how hard I push it." To draw on the metaphor, depending on Pablo's goal, the coach may ask pertinent possibility questions, such as:

- "With what are you pushing that wall?"
- "What else may help you push it?"
- "What does it usually take for you to move walls?"
- "What may happen if you stop pushing?"
- "What do you want to see on the other side of the wall?"
- "How does pushing help you?"
- "What will things be like when the wall crumbles?"

Such questions not only help clients reframe and reappraise their situation. Metaphors are a way for people to articulate their thoughts and emotions more easily or descriptively. Coaches' use of clients' metaphors in this way sometimes serves to lighten things up for clients.

If clients do not suggest metaphors themselves, coaches may ask questions that invite them to describe situations, emotions and other aspects of their conflict in metaphorical terms. This may mean picking up on something the client says to see whether a metaphor or other symbol resonates.

For example, if a client says, "There's something missing for me about the way Sophia apologized," the coach's possibility question could use a metaphor such as, "If she were making a cake, what ingredient would you say Sofia left out?" If this image resonates for the client, the coach may then continue the metaphor for that particular line of questioning and later in the coaching conversation, if appropriate. Generally speaking, though, metaphors that clients initiate are more effective because they are constructed from their own life experiences and associations.

Metaphors are just one creative way that coaches help clients to reappraise their situation by visualizing and experiencing their thoughts and feelings in different ways. For instance, some people refer to their situation or the other person within the context of a play, song, movie, television show, piece of art and so on. Other clients may initiate or respond to the coach's suggestion for another means to express themselves and make sense of their experience, such as by drawing a picture or writing a story, poem or song. An example follows.

A client in the car business once drew a vehicle to represent himself. In the drawing, the car had only three tires, and he used that and other pertinent symbols to describe how he felt after a disagreement with his boss. He then went on to describe how he was "running out of gas." Using these images was a fascinating and helpful way for him to describe how he was experiencing the dispute. What he needed to do to rebuild his "car" became his metaphoric goal.

Acknowledging Clients

Acknowledgments let clients know the coach hears, notices and understands their views, feelings, progress and woes. Acknowledging clients also assures them of the coach's support in their coaching journey.

Clients work hard to reach goals that require them to stretch their usual habits on many levels—emotional, intellectual, spiritual and behavioral. Coaches ask much of clients, and if they are doing their job well, they challenge them to think in different ways and to make meaningful changes in their lives. Even the fact that people step up to participate in the first place and make the effort to self-examine is significant. Coaches acknowledge clients throughout the coaching process, and there are many opportunities to do so as they gain insights, take steps forward, experience challenges and a range of emotions and so on. Acknowledging clients lets them know coaches care about them and their experiences. This does many things for clients, not the least of which is to inspire and motivate them.

Hand in hand with this topic of acknowledgment is the notion of extending appreciation to clients. Studies reveal that improved cognitive ability and performance are associated with a sustained state of appreciation, known also to reduce anxiety and stress.[5] Appreciation may be extended to clients for their efforts, for being candid, for sharing information, for engaging in a challenging process, for expressing their truth and emotions. It is also important that coaches understand and appreciate clients' resistances, blocks and concerns when they are not progressing and to celebrate their successes when they accomplish them.

Not all clients receive appreciation and acknowledgments well, and not all coaches are comfortable expressing support in this way. When clients react negatively to coaches' expressions of appreciation and acknowledgment, it is an opportunity for the coach to help them examine what is happening for them. When coaches find it challenging to extend support to clients sincerely and effectively, self-work is necessary.

Supporting Clients' Accountability

Accountability is a key component of coaching. Supporting clients' accountability means that coaches help clients benchmark and work toward accomplishing their goals—by ensuring that clients are developing action plans, moving forward and reaching their objectives. Accountability also means challenging and stretching clients to be who they strive to be and achieve what they want to achieve. This requires coaches to ensure that the process, the tasks, the timing and the coach–client relationship are working effectively to facilitate this success.

Clients' progress is the barometer, and when they do not progress the reasons warrant consideration. For example, the client may not have connected with the coach, the process or both. Clients may be emotionally entrenched in their conflict and not ready to move on; they may be blocked; or, they may be sabotaging themselves, the process or the coach owing to fear of failure or even fear of success. In any case, assessing progress is an ongoing function of coaches, and any apparent impediments to clients' forward movement are worthy of discussion about the reasons and what is required to overcome them.

Here are some ways for coaches to facilitate clients' accountability:

- Confirming clients know, from the beginning, that the coach's responsibility involves helping them keep accountable to do the work of coaching.
- Ascertaining, before coaching starts, how the client (and the organization, when applicable) will measure success.
- Ensuring that clients' goals for coaching are clear, attainable and measurable, and that target dates for accomplishing them are realistic.
- Collaborating on what the accountability measures will be and how they will be integrated into the process.
- Ensuring that clients are ready, willing and able to do the requisite work.
- Determining from clients what usually helps them reach their objectives and what impedes that from happening.
- Creating and continually building the rapport and trust that facilitates discussions on accountability.
- Reviewing clients' plans and goals on a regular basis.
- Monitoring and discussing with clients, on an ongoing basis, whether they are making progress according to the measurement(s) being used.
- Engaging clients supportively and positively in discussions about reasons they are not accomplishing what they intend, if that occurs.
- Acknowledging and appreciating clients' progress, insights, new learning and achievements.
- Remaining conscious of possible threats to clients' identity and status by the way coaches provide feedback.
- Remaining cognizant of whether clients are working on tasks between sessions and if not, finding out what is precluding them from doing so.

On this last point: as discussed in Chapter 4, there are different reasons that clients may not accomplish tasks between sessions. Rather than assume lack of commitment or accountability, the coach may find it useful to discuss this aspect within the larger context of the client's progress.

Conflict Competence[6]

Conflict management coaches see their share of unpredictable behaviors when working with clients in conflict: high emotions, blocks, fears, blaming, ruminating, victim stance and so on. The longer people are enveloped in their conflict-related emotions, the more challenging it is for clients to be future-focused and take steps to move forward.

Emotions that linger as a consequence of clients' situation may show up in different ways. For instance, some people take out their anger and related emotions about the other person and the situation on their coach. They may question the coach's skills, view the coach as a representative and agent of their organization and refuse to share relevant information owing to lack of trust about confidentiality. Other clients who are feeling rejected or upset by their conflict may, initially at least, be passive and unable to communicate well. These and many other responses of the human condition in conflict have the potential for overwhelming coaches who are not comfortable with clients' emotions, or if they are not conflict competent themselves.

Conflict competence refers to the knowledge, skills and ability to engage effectively in conflict and also to have the requisite proficiencies to assist others to do so. Conflict-competent coaches are self-reflective, emotionally and socially intelligent and adept at emotional regulation. Conflict management coaches also understand the necessity to model conflict competence in their personal and professional lives.

The significance of doing so extends beyond the obvious optics related to how coaches interact with clients, colleagues, bosses, co-workers, referral sources and others. Being conflict intelligent means that coaches do the self-work and build the awareness required to understand conflict and themselves within it. Strengthening their knowledge, skills and abilities through their own coaching better prepares coaches to understand and manage the various challenges of coaching clients through their conflicts. This helps coaches to manage clients' expectations and to separate themselves from clients' experiences.

Being conflict intelligent also means that coaches do not make judgments about how people "should" engage in conflict and do not impose their rule books on their clients. In this regard, conflict-intelligent coaches understand their own rule books and are able to identify and address their own needs such that they leave their own experiences, egos, assumptions, hopes and expectations out of clients' efforts to reach their goals.

Related to this discussion is the importance of concentrating on coaches' own caretaking and self-management. Developing a self-reflective practice is included in this part of the chapter on skills because it is an integral part of having a strong personal and professional foundation. Helping people, and especially those clients who are stressed about their conflicts and disputes, takes its toll on practitioners and can lead to burnout and "compassion fatigue."

Coaches, mediators, ombudsmen, HR professionals, psychologists, leaders, union representatives, lawyers and other practitioners who regularly work in the eye of conflict sometimes tend to take on the heavy weight of the conflicts that their clients carry. Signs of doing so to a degree that is excessive include finding it difficult to extricate oneself from clients' views and feelings, and routinely taking clients' experiences home. Some coaches become provoked by some clients, or lose patience, compassion and understanding. These and other adverse, overly personal or other reactions can have an impact on coaches' work and relationships with clients.

Doing the self-work to build and sustain a strong personal and professional conflict management foundation is critical for being a reflective practitioner, and includes not only being conflict competent and conflict intelligent. In addition to other areas for self-growth discussed so far, reflective practitioners also obtain their own coaching and supervision for the following purposes:

- To increase self-empathy and self-compassion.
- To examine tendencies that get in the way of remaining unattached to clients' emotions and outcomes.
- To be able to remain objective regarding clients' journeys and not make them their own.
- To increase conflict competence and resilience.

Being a self-reflective practitioner also requires coaches to assess themselves during and after coaching, to track areas that need development. Self-assessments are useful, too, when compared with clients' evaluations to see whether there are patterns that are identifiable by both client and coach. Chapter 7 discusses measuring conflict management coaching and includes components for clients to assess the process and the coach. The discussion here focuses primarily on coaches' learning and awareness.

What follows are examples of self-assessment forms for coaches that may be used in conjunction with conflict management coaching.

While Coaching Is in Progress

Figure 5.1 gives a sample coach self-assessment that can be used after every three or four sessions with a client.

FIGURE 5.1   COACH SELF-ASSESSMENT

Date: _____ Client: _____					
On a 5-point scale, 5 being "very" and 1 being "not at all":					
How centered and prepared am I before the coaching sessions begin?	1	2	3	4	5
Am I routinely on time?	1	2	3	4	5
Am I remaining present throughout?	1	2	3	4	5
How successful am I in getting into and maintaining the "flow" of the process?	1	2	3	4	5

How attached am I to the client's outcome?	1	2	3	4	5
How successful am I at leaving my ego, assumptions and needs out of the process?	1	2	3	4	5
How successful am I in staying on the client's goal and not shifting the focus to what I think may be a more suitable objective?	1	2	3	4	5
How successful am I at not leading the client, in other ways than above?	1	2	3	4	5
How successful am I at not becoming impatient or frustrated by the way my client is handling his/her situation?	1	2	3	4	5
How well am I following the model?	1	2	3	4	5

The places I am straying are:

_____

_____

_____

_____

How connected am I with my client?	1	2	3	4	5
How non-judgmental am I?	1	2	3	4	5
How empathetic and caring am I being?	1	2	3	4	5
How understanding, supportive, thoughtful and respectful am I being?	1	2	3	4	5
How strong is my rapport with the client?	1	2	3	4	5
How well do I manage the client's emotions?	1	2	3	4	5
How attentive and focused am I?	1	2	3	4	5
How effective am I at framing possibility questions?	1	2	3	4	5
How well am I listening and hearing this client?	1	2	3	4	5

To what degree am I overtalking?	1 2 3 4 5
How effective am I at providing observations and feedback to my client?	1 2 3 4 5
How much do I adhere to the principle of self-determination?	1 2 3 4 5
How satisfied overall do I feel with my skills?	1 2 3 4 5

The things that stood out most about what I am or am not doing in my relationship with this client are:

_____

_____

_____

_____

The points which I rated myself 3 or less in this assessment have to do with:

_____

_____

_____

_____

The point(s) that is (are) consistent with the feedback I am receiving from my client is (are):

_____

_____

_____

_____

The thing(s) I am learning from my work with this client that I intend to work on and apply to my next coaching session is (are):

_____

_____

_____

_____

The thing(s) that indicate that I require some work regarding my own conflict competence is (are):

_____

_____

_____

_____

Post-Coaching

After coaching is completed with a client, it is helpful for coaches to reflect back on self-assessments conducted throughout the process, such as the one in Figure 5.1. Figure 5.2 presents another self-assessment form that may be used at the end of coaching.

FIGURE 5.2   REFLECTING BACK

Date: _____

Date coaching completed: _____

Client: _____

1. When I think back on my work with this client, I did ____ did not ____ feel connected with him or her.

   If so, I think it was because:

   _____

   _____

   _____

   _____

   If not, it was likely because:

   _____

   _____

   _____

   _____

2. Some things I would have liked to have done differently with this client are:

_____

_____

_____

3. Some part(s) of the model that I seemed to have challenges with is (are):

_____

_____

_____

4. Some other things that seemed to be happening when I was coaching the client that I want to improve are:

_____

_____

_____

5. The things that appear to be a pattern that require some more work based on this and other clients are:

_____

_____

_____

6. The things I did well with this client and areas I have improved on are:

_____

_____

_____

7. The thing(s) that came up for me that I realize need work regarding how I manage conflict is (are):

_____

_____

_____

8. My plan of action for working on areas that require improvement:

My coaching:

_____

_____

My own conflict management:

_____

_____

Other thoughts and feelings:

_____

_____

Whether coaches use forms such as these or make notes after each session, or every three or four, on their own areas of development, some type of self-reflective practice is recommended. One-on-one supervision and coaching, or using peer groups, are effective ways for coaches to hold themselves accountable, to develop skills and to optimize their own potential. The importance of making such opportunities to do so and also to refine their techniques, improve client relationships and enhance conflict intelligence and competence as just discussed cannot be overstated.

Standards of Ethical Conduct for Conflict Management Coaches

The topic of ethical conduct for conflict management coaches is included in this chapter primarily because it is considered relevant to how coaches perform in their role. The specialty of conflict management coaching is still relatively new, and the development of more and different models will have an impact on the further evolution of a community of practice and specific standards of conduct.

Codes of ethical conduct provide guidelines for practitioners. Such documents also inform consumers of the standards that are considered

applicable to those providing the service. Coaching to date is unregu-
lated, and the International Coach Federation (ICF) and various other
coaching organizations and schools around the world provide principles
that address ethical conduct expected of their members. Consumers,
however, do not necessarily know which one(s) apply to their coach
in the event they are dissatisfied and have complaints. It is especially
confusing for the public, because many coaches have other professional affiliations and associated codes of conduct from other careers,
including psychologists, lawyers, mediators, ombudsmen, social workers and so on. What challenges consumers even more is that many
untrained people refer to themselves as coaches and have no educational or organizational affiliation to protect them or the public.

At the request of a number of organizations wanting its internal
coaches to adhere to a set of ethical principles, CINERGY™ developed a model Standards of Ethical Conduct in 2000, which has
been adapted further in recent years for other organizations. The
document reproduced in Figure 5.3 is based on the CINERGY™
model; the codes of ethics for the International Coach Federation,[7]
the International Association of Coaches[8] and the Association for
Coaching[9] were all helpful precedents. The provisions in this document apply to the workplace and may also be considered for conflict
management coaching in other contexts.

FIGURE 5.3   STANDARDS OF ETHICAL CONDUCT FOR CONFLICT MANAGEMENT COACHES

A. Definition

1. The purpose of these model Standards of Ethical Conduct for Conflict Management Coaches is:
   a. to provide standards of practice and principles for the conduct of conflict management coaches, also referred to as conflict coaches;
   b. to promote public confidence in conflict management coaching as a process for helping people enhance the way they engage in and manage conflict; and
   c. to inform clients, sponsors and the public of the model standards of practice and ethical requirements for providing conflict management coaching.

2. For the purpose of these model Standards of Ethical Conduct for Conflict Management Coaches:
   a. "Sponsor" in organizational/workplace coaching refers to the person, organization or entity that retains a conflict management coach on behalf of a staff member;
   b. "Client" refers to the person being coached;
   c. "Conflict management coach," also known as "conflict coach," refers to a person specifically trained to coach individuals to reach their conflict management goals; and
   d. "Conflict management coaching" or "conflict coaching" refers to a one-on-one voluntary process in which a trained coach supports and assists people to reach their goals for managing and resolving disputes, for preventing unnecessary conflict and for enhancing their conflict competency. The conflict management coaching process is essentially a conversation in which clients choose the goal(s) and coaches use a structure and range of skills for helping clients reach them. Conflict management coaching is not counseling or therapy.

B. Self-Determination

3. Conflict management coaches:
   a. Honor the guiding principle of self-determination;
   b. Understand and operate on the basis that the responsibility for the outcome of coaching is the clients', being based on their particular objectives, motivations and selected plans of action;

c. Respect and support clients' right and ability to select the options and solutions that work for them in their efforts to reach their goals;

d. Do not advise clients how to manage and solve their disputes and conflict; and

e. Know when to refer clients to other services, resources and relevant information.

C. Dignity, Respect and Courtesy

4. Conflict management coaches treat all clients with dignity, respect and courtesy.

5. Conflict management coaches demonstrate respect for clients' values, civil and human rights, culture, religion, gender, age, ethnicity, sexual orientation, disability and so on.

D. Non-Judgmental and Impartial

6. Conflict management coaches remain non-judgmental about clients and the issues they raise. They also remain impartial about any other person or persons who may be involved in the client's dispute or conflict.

E. Voluntariness

7. Conflict management coaches honor the principle that conflict management coaching is a voluntary process and that clients may choose to terminate the process.

8. Conflict management coaches shall ensure proper closure with the clients, in circumstances when they themselves choose to terminate the process such as when (a) they do not believe they are able to remain non-judgmental about their clients and their issues and/or to remain impartial about the other person or persons; (b) they do not believe they are sufficiently competent to provide conflict management coaching; (c) they realize that mental instability, substance abuse or other reasons impede clients' active participation in the process; (d) there is a conflict of interest or one may be perceived that precludes the coach's effectiveness and/or the clients' trust; (e) personal issues impair or interfere with the coach's performance; and/or (f) it is evident that the client is not benefiting from the process or indicates he or she has lost faith in the coach or the coaching process.

F. Confidentiality

9. Conflict management coaches respect the confidentiality of the information that clients share, unless: (a) disclosure is authorized in writing, by the clients; (b) clients reveal an intent of harm to themselves or others; (c) the information is required for educational and statistical purposes (in which event no names or identifiable information will be used); and/or (d) it is required by any applicable law(s) and court order.

10. When notes are maintained by conflict management coaches, they shall store or dispose of them in a way that ensures confidentiality and privacy and that also complies with any applicable organizational policies and legislation.

11. Conflict management coaches ensure that they verbally, or by way of a written document or agreement, confirm with clients and sponsors the terms and limitations of confidentiality before coaching begins.

12. In some cases, reporting back to the sponsor may be required as part of the conflict management coaching retainer/contract. In this event, the client participates in the disclosure and its content.

13. Conflict management coaches obtain agreement from clients and sponsors before providing their names as references.

G. Conflicts of Interest

14. Conflict management coaches will not purposely put themselves in a situation in which there is a potential or actual conflict between their interests and the interests of sponsors or clients who request their services.

15. Conflict management coaches will reveal any known affiliation that may cause a perception or actual conflict of interest or bias, discuss it with the client and sponsor when applicable and remove themselves from the process, if requested or appropriate.

16. If conflict management coaches become aware of a potential or actual conflict between their interests and the interests of a client, they will disclose it to the client and defer to the client's (and when applicable, the sponsor's) preferred way of managing it.

17. If there is a chance that conflict management coaches may be requested to be the coach for the other person in a client's dispute or conflict, they will advise prospective clients when they first meet that this possibility exists. If this situation does arise, conflict management coaches will not share any confidences conveyed to them by either of the clients.

H. Professional Conduct

18. Conflict management coaches:
    a. Do not overstate their qualifications, expertise or experience;
    b. Conduct themselves in a manner that reflects positively upon the fields of professional coaching and conflict management;
    c. Do not promise or suggest specific results from the conflict management coaching process;
    d. Do not knowingly exploit any aspect of their relationship with clients for their personal, professional or financial benefit beyond what remuneration they may receive for providing conflict management coaching;
    e. Are responsible for establishing clear and appropriate boundaries regarding physical contact with clients;
    f. Will ensure before coaching begins that, in addition to confirming terms and limitations of confidentiality, clients and sponsors understand their respective roles and responsibilities and what conflict management coaching is and is not;
    g. When applicable, will ensure their compensation, billing schedule and any other terms of their retainer are confirmed in advance of commencing coaching;
    h. Only take credit for their own work and do not copy others' research, work or materials without written authorization from the originating source;
    i. Continue to participate in training and other developmental initiatives to further develop and sustain their knowledge, skills and abilities as a provider of conflict management coaching; and
    j. Engage in coaching as needed to develop and sustain their own conflict intelligence and competence.

SUMMARY

- There are many skills that practitioners bring to conflict management coaching and many others that they further develop to assist clients in their efforts to reach their conflict management goals. Understanding and adhering to the model's framework and philosophy, employing reflective questions, using intuition as they follow clients on their coaching journeys, being comfortable with and able to work with the range of emotions that people in conflict may be experiencing are just a few of the fundamental skills that coaches employ to help clients find their way through their conflicts and disputes.

- Building and sustaining a rapport with clients is a necessary foundation for providing a forum in which they may thrive and progress. Such a milieu alleviates tension and is conducive to problem-solving, creativity, positivity and the inspiration to do the required work of coaching. A trusting connection with clients also facilitates the process of providing feedback and observations, which are critical components of effective coaching.

- Coaches, mediators and other conflict management professionals, leaders, HR professionals, lawyers and others who work with people in conflict do not always engage in self-reflective work to strengthen their own conflict management knowledge, skills and abilities. To provide conflict management coaching effectively, practitioners gain and strengthen their own conflict competence and intelligence.

- The skills of conflict management coaches are connected to complying with standards that support ethical practice. Because the specialty of conflict management coaching is relatively new, an official code of ethical conduct specific for practitioners has yet to be developed. The model Standards of Ethical Conduct for Conflict Management Coaches (Figure 5.3) suggests a number of guidelines for this coaching niche.

Notes

1. See, e.g., William Bergquist, "The Application of Appreciative Perspectives to the Coaching Enterprise," *International Journal of Coaching in Organizations* 4 (2007): 44–54; David L. Cooperider and Diana Whitney, *Appreciative Inquiry: A Positive Revolution in Change* (San Francisco: Berrett-Koehler, 2005); and Suresh Srivasta, *Appreciative Management and Leadership: The Power of Positive Thought and Action in Organizations* (San Francisco: Jossey-Bass, 1999).

2. Ellen Weber, "Do Your Questions Compel Others to Answer?" (December 9, 2010). *Brain Leaders and Learners,* http://www.brainleadersandlearners.com/ellen-weber/ two-footed-questions-for-innovative-results/.

3. David Rock and Linda J. Page, *Coaching with the Brain in Mind: Foundations for Practice* (Hoboken, NJ: John Wiley & Sons, 2009), 358.

4. *Ibid.*, 253.

5. Roger Fisher and Daniel Shapiro, *Beyond Reason: Using Emotions as You Negotiate* (New York: Penguin Group, 2005), 220, referring to studies from the Institute of HeartMath.

6. Books on this topic by authors Craig Runde and Tim Flanagan: *Becoming a Conflict Competent Leader: How You and Your Organization Can Manage Conflict Effectively* (San Francisco: Jossey-Bass, 2007); *Building Conflict Competent Teams* (San Francisco: Jossey-Bass, 2008); and *Developing Your Conflict Competence: A Hands-On Guide for Leaders, Managers, Facilitators, and Teams* (San Francisco: Jossey-Bass, 2010).

7. International Coach Federation, http://www.coachfederation.org/ about-icf/ethics/icf-code-of-ethics/.

8. International Association of Coaching, http://www.certifiedcoach.org/ index.php/about_iac/iac_code_of_ethics/.

9. Association for Coaching, http://www.associationforcoaching.com/ about/about02.htm.

CHAPTER 6

Applications of Conflict Management Coaching

Apart from coaching people on a one-on-one basis to gain increased competence to manage their interpersonal disputes independently, other applications of the CINERGY™ model have evolved. This chapter outlines several ways to apply the coaching model and its concepts for the purpose of helping people to engage more effectively in their conflicts and disputes in various forums.

Mediation Coaching

Some differences between coaching and mediation appear in Appendix II. Though they are different processes, conflict management coaching may be integrated within mediation. This section of the chapter considers several possible approaches to mediation coaching, including (a) pre-mediation, (b) during mediation and (c) post-mediation. The specific applications to be discussed are:

- When the parties have their own coach, neither of whom is the mediator.
- When the mediator coaches both parties.

Pre-Mediation Coaching

Pre-mediation coaching refers to a process in which practitioners hold separate meetings to prepare each disputant to participate in mediation as a consequence of an altercation that has already occurred. Not all mediators conduct pre-mediation sessions, and there are some who subscribe to the view that meeting parties privately prior to or even during mediation may bias the mediator about one of the parties or the issues in dispute.[1] Some other commentators have expressed concerns about the possibility of violating confidentiality and abuse of power.[2] The use of pre-mediation coaching described here considers the differences between having a coach for each party and the mediator providing coaching for both persons in dispute.

The circumstances in which most of the following points apply include interpersonal conflicts and disputes between co-workers or managers and their staff in the workplace, between life and business partners, between and among family members (for example, in settling estate issues) and in other matters in which communication and maintaining relationships are important to the dynamic.

Similarities

There are some similarities between the practitioners' roles when pre-mediation is conducted by coaches—one for each party*—and those mediators who conduct separate pre-mediation sessions with the parties before bringing them together for the joint session. For example, both coaches and mediators:

- Aim to build rapport and trust.
- Ensure that their particular roles and responsibilities are clear.
- Encourage the parties to do some preparatory work to be ready for the joint mediation session(s).
- Acknowledge that self-determination is an operating principle.
- Use some common skills, such as active listening.
- Communicate terms regarding voluntariness and confidentiality pertaining to their respective role and process.
- Aim to create a cooperative working relationship and environment.

Figure 6.1 outlines a number of factors in comparing pre-mediation sessions by a coach for each party and by mediators who conduct pre-mediation meetings. These are general comparisons only, given that pre-mediation practices vary as do types of mediation and mediators' styles. However, experience suggests that because mediators hear both sides of the dispute, and are required to be impartial in their role, they are precluded from exploring both parties' plans for the interaction and other related matters as extensively and comprehensively as a coach for each party.

---

* While it may be optimal for each party to have his or her own coach, this is not always feasible or cost efficient.

FIGURE 6.1   GENERAL COMPARISONS BETWEEN PRE-MEDIATION SESSIONS AS A COACH FOR A PARTY AND AS THE MEDIATOR

Pre-Mediation Coaching as a Coach Only (Who Is Not the Mediator)	Pre-Mediation Meetings as the Mediator
Purpose of pre-mediation	
Generally speaking, pre-mediation coaching concentrates more on conflict management than dispute resolution. That is, the main purpose is more focused on the client's goals with respect to managing the relationship dynamic and preparing the client to engage effectively in the process. This commonly entails helping the party to communicate viewpoints effectively, including what he or she wants to achieve in mediation, to regulate and manage emotions that may preclude a constructive interaction and to consider how to prepare to receive and respond to what the other person may say.	Generally speaking, mediators who conduct pre-mediation meetings concentrate more on dispute resolution than conflict management. The main purpose is to prepare parties for mediation by helping them understand the process, the provisions of the Agreement to Mediate including terms of confidentiality, and the roles and responsibilities of the parties and the mediator. Also, many mediators who conduct pre-mediation spend time listening to each party discuss his or her side of the situation and share his or her needs, hopes and expectations. Practitioners often encourage each party to consider, in advance of the joint meeting, the possible settlement options and the criteria for assessing mutually acceptable choices.
Confidentiality	
Coaching pre-mediation sessions are confidential, subject to exceptions that are outlined in a written or verbal agreement.	Mediator pre-mediation sessions are confidential, subject to exceptions that are usually outlined in a written agreement.

Feedback	
The coach provides feedback and observations to the client about his or her style of communication as he or she practices what to say and how to respond to the other person.	The mediator does not typically engage each person in a rehearsal of what he or she will say in the process or, if so, not typically to the extent that coaches do. If the mediator does discuss communication, the input is commonly instructional or advisory in nature.
Perspective-taking	
The coach typically helps the client analyze his or her perspective on the conflict, on the client him-/herself and on the other person. The coach also assists the client to explore the possible perspectives of the other person on the conflict and the relational dynamic.	The mediator asks each party to share his or her perspective on the issues in dispute, the dynamic between them or both. The mediator may also ask each party to discuss any thoughts on the other person's perspectives on the issues. Within the mediation itself, the mediator facilitates a discussion in which the parties share their perspectives with each other.
Number of pre-mediation sessions	
There is usually a series of coaching sessions.	There is typically one pre-mediation session, if any (though there has been a reported increase in some areas and types of mediation).
Impartiality	
Coaches champion and support the party they are coaching. They remain impartial about the other person in the dispute.	Mediators remain impartial about both parties in the dispute.

An important consideration regarding the role of coaches who provide pre-mediation coaching is to ensure that they do not interfere with the mediator's role. The coach's role is not to replace or duplicate the role that the mediator plays in pre-mediation or the mediation itself. If there is a possibility of overlap or the roles are unclear, it is necessary for the practitioners to connect and confirm their respective functions and their role in relation to the parties and the process.

Application of the CINERGY™ Model in Pre-Mediation Coaching

A suggested starting point to focus the parties and prime them to participate in mediation is to have them complete a preparatory form such as the one shown in Figure 6.2. Depending on the situation and whether a mediator or a coach uses the document, and the practitioner's role in the process, not all questions necessarily apply.

FIGURE 6.2   PREPARING FOR MEDIATION

One of the best ways to prepare for mediation is to consider in advance what is important to you and also what may be important to the other person. The questions below are helpful in this regard, and I would appreciate your answering them, please, before we meet. This information is CONFIDENTIAL.

Goal: What assistance do you want to help prepare you for the upcoming mediation?

_____

_____

_____

_____

_____

Please list three main points that you want to ensure I hear about your perspective on the dispute. (You will have a chance to tell me more when we meet.)

• _____

• _____

• _____

What do you care about most right now as you consider the upcoming mediation?

_____

_____

_____

_____

_____

What don't you know about the other person or his or her perspective that would help you to discuss your differences more effectively and/or reconcile them?

_____

_____

_____

_____

_____

MY PERSPECTIVE	THE OTHER PERSON'S PERSPECTIVE
What will success in this situation look like for you regarding: The issues in dispute? The relationship? Other (please specify):	What might success look like for the other person regarding: The issues in dispute? The relationship? Other (please specify):
On a scale of 1 to 10 (10 being "very much"), how important are the successes you indicated above? Issues: 1 2 3 4 5 6 7 8 9 10 Relationship: 1 2 3 4 5 6 7 8 9 10 Other: 1 2 3 4 5 6 7 8 9 10	What is your sense of how important the successes are for the other person as you indicated above, on the same 1 to 10 scale? Issues: 1 2 3 4 5 6 7 8 9 10 Relationship: 1 2 3 4 5 6 7 8 9 10 Other: 1 2 3 4 5 6 7 8 9 10

If you had the chance to relive the interaction(s) that you had with the other person, what would you say/do differently?	What could the other person have said or done differently in the dispute?
When you meet with the other person in the mediation, what may provoke you that he or she may say or do? How do you want to respond in order to keep the discussion conciliatory?	What may you say or do that could provoke the other person? What will you *not* do/say because you are aware it would be unproductive?

How do you want to be perceived during the mediation process (tone, manner, etc.)?

_____

_____

_____

_____

_____

What are you willing to apologize for, forgive, accept and/or do without resentment regarding the matter between you?	What are you hoping the other person may be willing to apologize for, forgive, accept and/or do without resentment regarding the matter between you?

What could the other person say or do to help you obtain closure in this dispute?

_____

_____

_____

_____

What is something you could say or do to help the other person obtain closure in this dispute?

_____

_____

_____

_____

What else do you want me to know about you that will assist me in my role to prepare you to participate actively in the mediation process?

_____

_____

_____

_____

Thank you very much. I look forward to our conversation.

Having initially spent some time on these or other, similar preliminary questions, pre-mediation coaching by a coach for each party may then follow the stages of the CINERGY™ model, based on the client's goals for coaching. The process and steps, as in the usual course, help clients focus their intentions, reflect on what they will do and say and otherwise prepare for the interaction. Mediators using the model conduct the steps to the extent feasible and necessary to remain an impartial facilitator.

During Mediation

The role of the coach may also be extended from the behind-the-scenes function to involve each party's coach attending the mediation. As may be expected, coaches do not act as spokespeople, advocates or representatives. Rather, the objectives of this role are:

- To support the client during the process.
- To help the client participate effectively and learn from the process.

- To assist the client if he or she is not interacting and communicating in ways that are consistent with his or her stated conflict management goals.
- To observe the client interact in a conflictual situation and provide ongoing assistance regarding related skills and approaches. (Such assistance may occur between mediation sessions if there are more than one; or, post-mediation may be provided, as will be discussed shortly.)

Whether and how coaches participate in the actual mediation involves a discussion among the parties, the coaches and the mediator. It is suggested that because the mediator manages the process, the way and extent to which coaches are involved during the mediation are ultimately the mediator's to decide. Considerations include:

- The parties' preferences when both have a coach, including whether the coaches remain in the mediation room or are otherwise available to discuss matters pertinent to their role.
- Whether the coaches, if present in the mediation room, may ask for a private meeting with their client and if so, under what circumstances.
- If only one person has a coach, whether the coach attends the mediation and if so, under what conditions.
- The mediator's role in pre-mediation compared with the coaches' role.
- How the mediator and coach(es) may best work together to ensure that the disputants participate in the process effectively and engage in the interaction according to their objectives.
- How to proceed if one or both parties have legal or union representation or another support person in attendance.

If coaches for each party attend the mediation, experience suggests they be silent partners in the joint meeting room itself and they otherwise work with their individual clients when the mediator calls for private meetings with each party (referred to as a caucus). Mediators who use caucuses shuttle between two rooms and, among other things, explore with each party separately the issues in dispute and the settlement options. These private meetings also serve to break the tension and help each party process information gained and his or her emotional responses.

When the mediator calls a caucus and the parties are with their coaches, he or she may also make observations regarding unproductive interactions. The coaches then work privately with their clients regarding their interaction with the other person based on their own observations and those brought to the caucus by the mediator. Time required, and other considerations for resuming joint sessions, remains under the purview of the mediator.

Coaches also work with their client between sessions, if there are more than one, regarding the client's conflict management communication style and any responses requiring attention in the mediation.

Post-Mediation Coaching

Post-mediation coaching is a voluntary and confidential process that one or both parties may choose to participate in after mediation has ended. Common purposes of conflict management coaching under these circumstances are to help the client to focus and work on goals, such as:

- To continue to develop the relationship with the other person.
- To consider how to address any unmet or unresolved issues that may become apparent after the process begins.
- To reconcile disappointment and other negative emotions when there is an unsatisfactory resolution of the issues and relationship.
- To concentrate on certain skills identified by the client as requiring development to engage in future conflict more effectively.
- To improve conflict resilience.

People who retain coaches for pre-mediation assistance may choose to continue to see the coach for these or other purposes post-mediation.

Or, sometimes individuals seek coaching assistance only when they recognize the need to develop their conflict management skills in the aftermath of a mediation. For that matter, this type of coaching may be used after other ADR processes by any participants who want assistance with the same or other objectives. At this time, it is not a usual function of mediators to provide post-mediation coaching for one or both parties.

As an Option in Integrated Conflict Management Systems

A systems approach for developing conflict-competent workplaces is known as an Integrated (or Informal) Conflict Management System (ICMS).[3] The growth of this specialized area of organizational development is due in large part to the high financial and other costs of poorly managed conflict. A well-designed ICMS helps to create an organizational culture that, among other things, provides the ways and means for leaders and other staff to obtain ready assistance in managing discordant situations as soon as they become apparent. Typical objectives of an ICMS include:

- To build conflict-competent workplaces.
- To increase retention and productivity.
- To decrease absenteeism due to conflict-related stress.
- To reduce litigation and complaints that may be addressed in more conciliatory and less costly ways.
- To improve workplace interrelationships and morale.

Systems that accomplish such goals support and implement a range of services that give employees optional mechanisms for handling interpersonal workplace conflicts and disputes.

In designing the system and the options that are appropriate for their leaders' and employees' needs, workplaces usually consider interpersonal conflicts between and among co-workers and those between managers and their direct reports. Conflict with consumers of an organization's products or services, when applicable, may also be contemplated in a systems approach.

Methods to address workplace disputes consider the spectrum of possible conflicts, from matters relating to counterproductive communication to statutory-based complaints. A range of interest-based processes, such as mediation and facilitated dialogue, are made available, as are rights-based interventions such as arbitration. The scope is meant to provide workplaces with easily accessible self-help techniques at one end of the continuum and at the other end, a process through which a third party or panel makes a decision to resolve issues in dispute.

Since the 1990s, ICMS programs have been offering conflict management coaching as an option to staff in various countries, including Canada, Australia and the United States. To date, the conflict management coaching process is known to assist leaders and other staff in gaining conflict competence to manage interpersonal conflicts and disputes without third-party intervention. It is also used as a pre-mediation technique and to coach managers and supervisors to conduct effective performance reviews and other conversations expected to be contentious.[4]

As Part of Conflict Management Training

HR professionals, managers, school principals and others in leadership positions within private and public sector organizations often take courses specifically to learn conflict management skills and techniques including how to mediate and coach staff to resolve interpersonal disputes. Other types of conflict management training in workplaces may include teaching managerial and non-managerial staff to conduct peer mediation or peer conflict management coaching. In addition, employees who work with the public are trained to manage customer complaints and disputes.

When organizations determine which staff are suitable for training, they typically consider variables such as the optimal duration of training, the most useful content and assessing the relevance and sustainability of the learning. The fundamental question is: What training yields the best return on investment?

In recognition of research on how follow-up coaching significantly optimizes training,[5] this application of conflict management coaching suggests a model for both pre-training and post-training coaching to enhance and sustain conflict management training.

Purposes of Pre-Training Meetings

The purposes for coach-trainers to conduct pre-training meetings with participants prior to conflict management workshops are:

- To determine each person's conflict challenges.
- To consider the overall themes presented by the participants regarding areas requiring development.
- To plan the content and experiential exercises so that the training is specific to the needs of those attending.
- To gain an understanding of the organizational culture of the participants.
- To ascertain whether an assessment tool may be beneficial as part of the training and if so, which one.
- To begin the process of coaching by increasing each participant's self-awareness about developmental areas relating to his or her conflict management skills and abilities.
- To build a foundation for an ongoing relationship in the training and post-training.

As is evident from this list of purposes, pre-training meetings provide coach-trainers with the opportunity to customize various aspects of the conflict management training program to meet the specific needs of the audience. Participants appreciate being a part of the plans for their learning and development, and they approach workshops with a clearer identification of which of their skills require strengthening.

Up to 120 minutes per person is recommended for individual pre-training sessions. Experience suggests that two one-hour meetings per person is an approach that works well.

Purposes of Post-Workshop Conflict Management Coaching

The overall intention of post-training coaching is to help participants embed their new knowledge and skills and further develop their conflict competence. The other purposes of post-workshop coaching are:

- To help participants implement their individual action plans for developing their conflict management skills.
- To support their efforts to apply new skills and awareness to the specific challenges they encounter after the training.
- To ensure that participants are gaining increased confidence and competence for carrying out the learned skills.

Experience has shown that a minimum of six post-workshop coaching sessions of approximately one hour in length over a three- to six-month period support this purpose. Group coaching may be used instead of, or in combination with, individual coaching.

Collaborative Law

Collaborative law (CL) is a dispute resolution model in which each party retains a specially trained lawyer and together, the parties and their counsel collaborate in negotiations to resolve the issues in dispute. In this process, which has grown significantly in the area of family law, the participants agree to work jointly in good faith and to make their best efforts to find "win–win" solutions that respect and acknowledge the interests of both parties. Further, the lawyers and clients undertake that neither party may go to court as long as the disputants are attempting to settle matters this way.

If issues remain unsettled using the CL process, it terminates and both legal counsel are disqualified from going to court as representatives of the clients who retained them. Such a process is meant, in part, to reduce the adversarial nature of the parties' legal differences. It empowers clients to be more directly involved and active in their settlement discussions and to work toward conciliatory and cooperative interactions and outcomes.

Coaching within this forum by the parties' lawyers, or by a coach, accomplishes at least two objectives:

- To prepare parties to participate effectively and actively in the negotiations about the issues in dispute in CL meetings.
- To increase the parties' comfort and confidence in interacting with the other person for the longer term.

The purpose of coaching aligns with the concept of collaborative negotiation by enabling the parties to participate actively and effectively in the joint sessions. The individualized process helps clients prepare to identify and state their issues and interests to the other person. Through coaching, the parties think out and prepare to convey messages they expect to be challenging and to be ready to receive viewpoints and reactions that may be difficult.

When coaching is conducted by lawyers, this application also helps them to prepare for CL joint meetings by anticipating the inter-relationship matters that will require attention at the joint meeting. Another objective of conflict management coaching in this context is to prepare lawyers to anticipate and manage possible challenges between themselves and other counsel.

SUMMARY

- Conflict management coaching is an individualized process for helping people better manage their disputes and gain conflict competence and is broadly applicable. More applications are likely to develop as the synergies between the ADR and coaching fields expand.

- Several applications of conflict management coaching currently in use include preparing people to participate in Alternative Dispute Resolution processes such as mediation. It may also be used after people have participated in an ADR forum to provide further assistance regarding their skills and abilities to engage in conflict. Further, as an adjunct to general conflict management training, this form of coaching helps participants sustain and embed their learning.

- Increasingly, mediators who are trained as coaches, and coaches who are trained as mediators, are combining their skills to provide more extensive coaching for disputants prior to and during the mediation process.

Notes

1. For more discussion on the use of pre-mediation, see, e.g., Christopher W. Moore, "The Caucus: Private Meetings That Promote Settlement," *Mediation Quarterly* 16 (Summer 1987): 87–101; Gregorio Billikopf-Encina, "Contributions of Caucusing and Pre-Caucusing to Mediation," *Group Facilitation: A Research and Applications Journal* 4 (Spring 2002): 3–11; and Joyce Odidison, *Getting Ready for Mediation: A Pre-Mediation Concept* (Winnipeg: Interpersonal Wellness Services, 2004).

2. Concerns expressed in the literature include the possibility of violation of confidentiality by the mediator and abuse of power by mediators. See, in the first instance, Christopher W. Moore, *The Mediation Process: Practical Strategies for Resolving Conflict* (San Francisco: Jossey-Bass, 2003) and, in the second, Joan Blades, "Mediation: An Old Art Revitalized," *Mediation Quarterly* 16 (March 1984): 15–19.

3. Related texts on the concept of ICMS: David B. Lipsey, Ronald L. Seeber and Richard Fincher, *Emerging Systems for Managing Workplace Conflict: Lessons from American Corporations for Managers and Dispute Resolution Professionals* (San Francisco: Jossey-Bass, 2003); Allan Stitt, *Alternative Dispute Resolution for Organizations: How to Design a System for Effective Conflict Resolution* (Toronto: John Wiley & Sons Canada, 1998); Cathy A. Costantino and Christina Sickles Merchant, *Designing Conflict Management Systems: A Guide to Creating Productive and Healthy Organizations* (San Francisco: Jossey-Bass, 1996); William Ury, Jeanne M. Brett and Stephen B. Goldberg, *Getting Disputes Resolved: Designing Systems to Cut the Costs of Conflict* (San Francisco: Jossey-Bass, 1988); and Karl A. Slaikeu and Ralph H. Hasson, *Controlling the Costs of Conflict: How to Design a System for Your Organization* (San Francisco: Jossey-Bass, 1988).

4. See, e.g., Treasury Board of Canada Secretariat, "Getting to Know Informal Conflict Management Systems (ICMS) Better," http://www.tbs-sct.gc.ca/gui/conflplus-eng.asp; Cinnie Noble, Sam Slosberg and Scott Becker, "Conflict Management Coaching at the Transportation Security Administration" (October 2009), *Mediate.com*, http://www.mediate.com/articles/nobleC11.cfm; Helen Marks, "Results Through People" (August 2005), *Australian Government Department of Defence Magazine*; and State Government of Victoria State Services Authority, "Developing Conflict Resilient Workplaces: A Report for Victorian Public Sector Leaders" (2010), http://www.ssa.vic.gov.au/products/view-products/developing-conflict-resilient-workplaces.html.

5. Gerald Olivero, Denise K. Bane and Richard E. Kopelman, "Executive Coaching as a Transfer of Training Tool: Effects on Productivity in a Public Agency," *Public Personnel Management* 26 (Winter 1997) (4): 461–69.

Measuring Conflict Management Coaching

As conflict management coaching and its applications continue to evolve, measuring its impact is integral to establishing its legitimacy and inspiring its use. This chapter suggests variables for coaches, clients and organizations to consider in their efforts to determine the success of conflict management coaching from their various perspectives. Though the focus here is the organizational context, most ideas may be extrapolated to assess a range of measurement factors in other situations. Regardless of the context, whichever criteria are selected for assessment depend on the purpose of the evaluation, who and what is being evaluated and how the results will be used.

Variables to Consider

From an organizational point of view, the variables to be assessed regarding measurement of conflict management coaching include:

- Whether there is a return on investment.
- The client's progress and success at attaining his or her coaching goals.
- Any identifiable qualitative benefits, including the impact of coaching on the client and on others who work with him or her.
- The number of staff members using the process.
- The nature of the interpersonal workplace conflicts and disputes for which staff seek coaching.
- Who is using the service (managers, non-managers).
- Whether the person being coached was referred for assistance or requested it.
- The client's satisfaction with the process.
- The client's satisfaction with the coach.

Return on Investment

Typically, a primary goal of organizations when instituting new services is to justify the expense of retaining external coaches, training internal staff and developing a conflict management coaching program. The main question—"Will it save us money?"—entails a cost–benefit analysis to determine whether there is a return on investment (ROI) from conflict management coaching.[1]

Many indicators of poorly managed conflict may be benchmarked and used as criteria for determining cost implications. Factors include the cost of related litigation, grievances and civil rights claims, the time spent by managers and co-workers on their staff's or colleagues' disputes, absenteeism, medical leave and retention problems arising from the stress of workplace conflict, decreased productivity and loss of business.

Another way to measure success in organizations is to keep statistics on the number of users of conflict management coaching. One consideration is whether there is an increase in staff who are obtaining help with their interpersonal disputes by availing themselves of coaching rather than more expensive options. Indirectly an ROI variable, the question of who uses the service (managers or non-managers) and their reasons for coming to coaching also informs organizations of what training and other processes may be needed to build a more conflict-competent workplace and reduce the costs of unmanaged disputes.

The bottom line when measuring the usefulness of a service is not only the financial one. As significant as that is to the organization, it is important to consider qualitative factors, which also reflect ROI. One of these is whether there is a positive result and impact, not only for the clients but also for their managers, co-workers, direct reports and others. Outcomes of this nature may include stronger leadership skills, improved interrelationships and morale among staff, productive disagreements, increased efforts to cooperate and other benefits.

Determining coaching objectives at the beginning of the process and how success will be measured helps to identify the criteria to be used. Monitoring clients' progress during coaching based on their stated goals, and following up on the durability and further application of their learning after coaching has stopped, are other possible ways to add a qualitative as well as a quantitative analysis.

Developing the appropriate criteria, and conducting assessments that provide sufficient information to evaluate the effectiveness of coaching specific to the organization's needs, require time and careful consideration. The forms and questionnaires in this chapter provide some suggestions from a range of perspectives and may be applied at different points in the coaching process.

The Client's Progress Toward Identifiable Goals

Clients' progress toward and success in attaining their stated goals may be assessed before, during and after coaching.

Before Coaching Begins

One way of encouraging clients to focus on their coaching objectives is to use a form like the one in Figure 3.5 (Chapter 3, page 104), "Preparing for Your First Coaching Session." Use of this form is optional; the coach could instead ask similar questions before the process begins, such as, "What are you hoping to achieve?," "How will you know if conflict management coaching is effective for you?" and "How will your manager, reports, co-workers and others know that conflict management coaching is working for you?" These examples provide both objective and subjective measurement criteria. Even a client's answer, "I won't feel sick to my stomach every day when I work with Tom!" is concrete and measurable.

Coaches do not always meet or speak with sponsors and clients together before coaching begins. However, when that occurs, ascertaining the objectives and indicators of success aims to obtain the specificity needed to measure progress. Initial discussions on measurement criteria may also consider whether other stakeholders ought to be engaged in discussions of this nature before coaching starts. Such inquiries may take various forms, from making informal requests for input to formal assessments (to be discussed later in this chapter).

During Coaching

Coaches regularly check in to assess clients' progress and ask them to reflect on and evaluate the effectiveness of coaching. In this regard, variables may include (a) whether clients perceive they are moving forward toward their goals, (b) how the coaching process itself is working for them and (c) how they experience the coach–client relationship.

Assessments of this nature may be done in written or discussion format on a periodic basis. The results serve to build in accountability and alert coaches to matters that are motivating or impeding progress.

ASSESSING CLIENTS' PROGRESS TOWARD THEIR GOALS

Using a form like the one in Figure 4.3 (Chapter 4, page 140), "Looking Forward," offers an ongoing opportunity to have clients assess their own progress after each session. Another assessment during the coaching process sometimes occurs if sponsors want to check in with the coach and client at some interim point, as suggested in Chapter 3. This is typically a chance for the sponsor to find out what progress is being made, to provide possible input on his or her observations and sometimes, to consider whether more coaching is required than previously contracted.

A further way for coaches to assess clients' coaching progress on a periodic basis is to use rating scales such as those in Figure 7.1. This form combines self-rating scales with narrative questions.

Questionnaires are not every coach's preferred method of conducting such assessments. However, when used, they may be designed to assess the factors suggested here and also ones that coaches and clients (and possibly, sponsors) determine together as progress variables. As with other questionnaires suggested in this chapter, an accompanying dialogue helps to focus on themes and concerns.

FIGURE 7.1 MY PROGRESS SO FAR

Please let me know how you are doing so far in your coaching experience by answering this brief questionnaire. This is a CONFIDENTIAL document.

Client: Date coaching started:

On a 5-point scale, with 5 being "absolutely yes" and 1 being "absolutely no," please circle how you rate your coaching progress so far, with respect to the following:

Pace
• I am moving at a good pace toward my goal.   1 2 3 4 5
• I would like to be moving at a faster pace.   1 2 3 4 5

I think the reason(s) I am not moving at a good pace (if applicable) is (are):

_____

_____

_____

I think the reason(s) I am moving at a good pace (if applicable) is (are):

_____

_____

_____

Impact

I am noticing improvements about how I manage conflict in the workplace as a consequence of coaching.   1 2 3 4 5

The improvements are as follows:

_____

_____

Impact on me:

_____

_____

_____

Impact on others:

_____

_____

_____

(If applicable:) The possible reason(s) there is not much improvement is (are):

_____

_____

_____

Optimism

I am optimistic that I will reach my goal.   1 2 3 4 5

I am optimistic because:

_____

_____

(If applicable:) I think the reason(s) I am not optimistic about reaching my goal is (are):

_____

_____

_____

_____

Insights

I am gaining insights that will help me reach my goal.   1 2 3 4 5

The insights from coaching that stand out right now are:

_____

_____

_____

(If applicable:) I think the reason(s) I am not gaining insights is (are):

_____

_____

_____

Other comments:

_____

_____

_____

_____

Thank you for completing this form. I'll appreciate it if you will please fax your responses to me at _____ or email me at _____ before our next session.

ASSESSING THE PROCESS

Coaches also regularly check in with clients to find out how the process itself is working for them. This factor may be included in the previous type of questionnaire using a rating scale, or it may be addressed during the related discussion. Whether or not forms are used, simple and straightforward questions that are narrative in nature work well, for example:

- What about the process do you find most effective?
- What is not as effective for you?
- What might work better?

Conversations with clients about these variables usually yield concrete ideas that give the client and coach the chance to further co-create an approach that might be more workable.

ASSESSING THE COACH–CLIENT RELATIONSHIP

Generally speaking, an assessment of the coach during the course of coaching is likely of greater concern to coaches than the organization. However, some organizations may at some point want input from clients on their coach's effectiveness.

Given that clients are on the receiving end of feedback throughout coaching, it is meaningful for them to be asked for their observations on the coach regarding how he or she is meeting their expectations. This approach models openness, and how the coach responds is significant for clients who may struggle with sharing their perspectives, especially if they have negative views about the coach.

Moreover, how clients respond when asked for their input sometimes reflects the challenges they may experience in offering feedback, especially if they have sought help in this area. In such cases, these discussions are coachable occasions for assisting clients to further explore their related conflict management goals.

Using forms and scales in assessing the coach–client relationship also works effectively, and the related line of inquiry may be included in the previous questionnaire (Figure 7.1). Experience suggests that asking clients to assess the relationship seems to work well when the coach periodically engages the client in a discussion that includes other topics, such as the coaching process.

Some useful and straightforward questions might include:

- What is working well for you that I do?
- What might I do to assist you more effectively?

- On a 10-point scale, 10 being "very much" and 1 being "not at all," how would you rate the degree to which you perceive I am hearing you? Understanding you?

At the time of this conversation, coaches may want to discuss their own impressions about the working relationship. In addition to expressing observations on clients' efforts, the coach will want to address any signs of clients' diminishing trust or interest in coaching, or other observations that signal concern about the process or relationship. (It is usual and optimal, however, if coaches raise such observations at the time they notice them.)

After Coaching

The end of coaching presents another opportunity to measure success. Variables at this time may include one or a combination of the following:

- The client's progress.
- Costs and benefits.
- The qualitative usefulness of the process.
- The coach's effectiveness.

Post-coaching assessments may be done at various times: (a) right at the end of coaching, (b) shortly (perhaps four to six weeks) after coaching ends and (c) several months after. Each assessment yields different information, both quantitatively and qualitatively. Being clear on the purpose of the assessment is key. In any case, the caution is to avoid inundating clients with too many assessments and to choose the one(s) that are most suitable for and relevant to the client and the organization.

Some suggestions follow for assessing clients in one or more of these three possible scenarios.

RIGHT AT THE END OF COACHING

Figure 7.2 gives an example of an optional questionnaire for clients immediately post-coaching that provides narrative data specifically related to their goals. This form suggests that the coach will also make a follow-up call to the client.

FIGURE 7.2   MEASURING GOAL ATTAINMENT

Thank you for participating in conflict management coaching. At this time, I would appreciate receiving your feedback on whether and how your coaching experience was effective for you with respect to your goals. Please complete the following CONFIDENTIAL form and return it to me within 10 days, if possible. I will follow up with a brief phone call (about 15 minutes) at your convenience. Thank you in advance for your input.

Name: _____ Date: _____

• When I began coaching, I stated my goal(s) to be:

_____

_____

_____

• The goal(s) I have reached is (are):

_____

_____

_____

• When I began coaching, I stated that I would measure my success by:

_____

_____

_____

• I achieved success in the following way(s):

_____

_____

_____

• The ways that others observe that I have been successful are:

_____

_____

_____

• The thing(s) I didn't achieve in coaching that I expected I would was (were):

_____

_____

_____

• The thing(s) I achieved in coaching that I didn't expect to is (are):

_____

_____

_____

Other comments:

_____

_____

_____

On completion of this form, please return it by fax to _____ or by email to _____. Thank you again. I will contact you in a few days to set up a time for a call.

SHORTLY AFTER COACHING

The questionnaire in Figure 7.3 is suggested as an evaluation that could be used by the coach or the organization four to six weeks after coaching ends. (Or, it may instead be used immediately following coaching.) This document lists specific questions for measuring success, costs and benefits, the process and the coach.

There is also a section on identifying the nature of conflict issues in the workplace. Needless to say, such information is compiled in a way that maintains anonymity of the client and the other person in the dispute. Similarly, the content of coaching is not disclosed.

FIGURE 7.3   ASSESSING COACHING

Thank you for taking a few minutes to let us know how the coaching process worked for you. This document is CONFIDENTIAL and will be used for compiling non-identifiable statistics and data on the use and effectiveness of coaching.

Number of coaching sessions: _____

Number of hours: _____

My first day of coaching was: _____

My last day of coaching was: _____

Please put a check mark beside whichever points apply to your conflict/dispute	✔

Goals My goals for coaching were: 1. To resolve/manage a past, current or future interpersonal dispute with a co-worker/boss/support staff/direct report/other (customer, client, etc.). [Please circle whichever position applies. If the other person's role is not indicated, please specify without naming him/her:] _____ _____ Please circle the applicable timeframe for the dispute: Past / Current / Future	
2. To increase my knowledge, skills and abilities to engage in conflict more effectively.	
3. To talk and think out my concerns about a past, current or future conflict or dispute. [Please circle the timeframe that applies: Past / Current / Future]	
4. To decide whether to do something about a conflict situation and if so, what that may be.	
5. To gain assistance about how to acknowledge and apologize for my contribution to an interpersonal dispute.	
6. To consider my options about a conflict situation.	

7. To prepare for mediation or other process for resolving a dispute.	
8. To gain help with the lingering effects of a previous dispute.	
9. To prepare for a challenging one-on-one conversation.	
10. To prepare for a contentious group/team meeting as the leader or participant. [Please circle whichever applies: Leader / Participant]	
11. To work on one or more of my responses to conflict that require improvement.	
12. Other (please specify without naming anyone): _____ _____ _____	
I achieved my specific goal(s): Yes____ No_____ In part____ If no or in part, I think the reason(s) is (are): _____ _____ _____	

Outcome(s) of Coaching

On a 5-point scale, with 5 being "absolutely yes" and 1 being "absolutely no," please circle the rating that reflects your response to the following statements. If you do not think a point applies to you, please circle N/A. Please add any comments you think might be useful on the points you have rated.

As a result of coaching:		Comments
1. I was able to manage my conflict situation more effectively than I would have without coaching.	1 2 3 4 5 N/A	

2. I was satisfied to have the opportunity to talk to someone who is objective and not judgmental.	1 2 3 4 5 N/A	
3. I gained increased insight and awareness that helped me better understand my conflict/dispute.	1 2 3 4 5 N/A	
4. I made a plan of action to resolve my conflict situation and have not acted on it yet.	1 2 3 4 5 N/A	
5. I made a plan of action to resolve my conflict situation and do not intend to proceed with it after all.	1 2 3 4 5 N/A	
6. I made a plan of action to resolve my conflict situation and acted on it, with success.	1 2 3 4 5 N/A	
7. I made a plan of action to resolve my conflict situation and acted on it, though it did not work out as well as I had hoped.	1 2 3 4 5 N/A	
8. I am told by others that I have improved the way I manage conflict. Please specify in what ways others have said you have improved:	1 2 3 4 5 N/A	
9. I made amends with the other person(s).	1 2 3 4 5 N/A	
10. I gained an understanding of what upset me in the conflict/dispute and what led to my reaction(s).	1 2 3 4 5 N/A	

11. I gained an understanding of my contribution to a conflict/dispute.	1 2 3 4 5 N/A	
12. I gained increased confidence to manage a conflict situation.	1 2 3 4 5 N/A	
13. I gained new skills and ways of coping and interacting when in conflict that I will apply in other situations.	1 2 3 4 5 N/A	
14. There is a reduction in the negative emotions I had about the other person and/or the situation.	1 2 3 4 5 N/A	
15. I am less stressed about the conflict.	1 2 3 4 5 N/A	
16. I made a positive change in my general approach and attitude to conflict that I am using or intend to use with future conflicts and disputes.	1 2 3 4 5 N/A	

If through conflict management coaching you experienced an outcome about your way of managing conflict, a particular situation and/or relationship other than the ways referred to above, please specify, without identifying the names or the substance of the conflict or dispute:

_____

_____

_____

_____

Other comments about the outcome of coaching:

_____

_____

_____

_____

The Coach

Using the same 5-point scale, 5 being "absolutely yes" and 1 being "absolutely no," please circle the number that reflects your response to the following statements about the coach. If any do not apply, please circle N/A.

The coach was:		Comments
1. Informative and clear about what coaching is, the model and process used, confidentiality, his/her role and my role.	1 2 3 4 5 N/A	
2. On time and available when I was, or otherwise accommodated my schedule as much as possible.	1 2 3 4 5 N/A	
3. A great listener.	1 2 3 4 5 N/A	
4. Skilled at helping me manage my emotions about my conflict/dispute and the other person.	1 2 3 4 5 N/A	
5. Non-judgmental and objective.	1 2 3 4 5 N/A	
6. Impartial about the other person(s) involved in my conflict/dispute.	1 2 3 4 5 N/A	
7. Understanding, supportive, thoughtful, respectful and empathetic.	1 2 3 4 5 N/A	
8. Trusting of me to decide for myself what to do and how to be able to reach my goal.	1 2 3 4 5 N/A	
9. Not leading me to outcomes that seemed to be more about what he/she wanted me to say/do than what I wanted to say/do.	1 2 3 4 5 N/A	

10. Focused on me and my goal throughout the process.	1 2 3 4 5 N/A	
11. Other (please be specific):	1 2 3 4 5 N/A	

Alternatives to Coaching

If I had not gone to coaching, I would have:			Comments *Please check whichever points apply*
1. Left the organization.	Yes	No	
2. Escalated the issue by: • Initiating or following through on a grievance, claim or other type of formal internal complaint. • Starting or following through on litigation. • Going above the other person's head. • Other (please specify):	Yes	No	
1. Taken (more) time off work for stress/medical leave.	Yes	No	
2. Asked for a transfer.	Yes	No	
3. Done nothing.	Yes	No	
4. Other (please specify):	Yes	No	

Recommending Coaching	Comments
I would recommend coaching to others: Yes____ No ____ If yes, why? If no, why not? 	
Other Information I was: Self-referred_____ Referred_____ I am: A Manager_____ Not a Manager_____	

Name (optional): _____

Coach's name: _____

Today's date (month/year): _____

Please return to _____ by fax to _____ or by email to _____.

More questions on any of the categories in the questionnaire in Figure 7.3 may, of course, be added. Similarly, external and internal coaches may extract parts of such questionnaires required or requested to measure the variables that the organization wants to assess and to retain parts that pertain to themselves or the process, unless these are also requested by the organization.

SEVERAL MONTHS POST-COACHING

Some coaches and organizations want to assess the durability of clients' learning gained through coaching. A common time to do so is four to six months after coaching ends. Like other evaluations, this may be done verbally, by questionnaire or by using a combination of both or other modes.

Figure 7.4 gives an example of a narrative-type questionnaire suitable for this purpose that is more in the nature of the types of questions that coaches ask.

FIGURE 7.4   FOLLOW-UP COACHING

I am interested to know about your coaching experience as you look back on it now. I would appreciate your taking a few minutes, please, to answer the following questions. Then, kindly return this CONFIDENTIAL document to me by email to _____ or fax to _____ by _____, if possible. Thank you very much.

Name: _____ Date: _____

Date coaching completed: _____

• What are your strongest memories about your coaching experience?

_____

_____

_____

• In what ways has your life improved by participating in conflict management coaching?

_____

_____

_____

(If applicable:) In what ways has your situation related to your conflict/dispute *not* improved since coaching? If so, what might be the reason(s) for this?

_____

_____

_____

• In what ways, if any, do you continue to apply your learning from conflict management coaching?

_____

_____

_____

• What awareness and learning that you gained in coaching, if any, have *not* been sustained? If so, what might be the reason(s)?

_____

_____

_____

- As you reflect back, if there are things I could have done to be more helpful, or if there is something about the process that could be improved upon, please feel free to share your suggestions:

_____

_____

_____

Other comments:

_____

_____

_____

I appreciate that you have taken time to complete this form. Thank you. If you have any questions, do not hesitate to contact me.

The next questionnaire in Figure 7.5 uses a rating scale and provides more specific data on the results of coaching. It is helpful both for coaches and for organizations that want to conduct a longer-term post-coaching evaluation. The form may be designed to include the particular areas that clients worked on in coaching and other relevant points, such as those from the previous questionnaires. At this juncture, short questionnaires are generally more effective.

FIGURE 7.5   SUSTAINABILITY OF THE COACHING EXPERIENCE

This form asks you to let me know what is sustained for you from your coaching experience on a scale of 1 to 5, 5 being "absolutely yes" and 1 being "absolutely no." If a factor is not applicable, please just mark it N/A. Please feel free to add any comments.	
Since my conflict management coaching, I:	
1. Continue to apply my learning to other conflict situations.	1 2 3 4 5 N/A
2. Am more confident about raising conflictual issues.	1 2 3 4 5 N/A

3. Have a more positive and optimistic view about conflict.	1 2 3 4 5 N/A
4. Have increased awareness and understanding of how I contribute to my interpersonal disputes.	1 2 3 4 5 N/A
5. Respond more effectively to conflict and better manage my reactions when I am in conflict.	1 2 3 4 5 N/A
6. Am generally less stressed when I encounter conflict situations.	1 2 3 4 5 N/A
7. Know I have choices about how to manage conflict and now select ones that are more effective than before I participated in coaching.	1 2 3 4 5 N/A
Other sustainable gains: _____ _____ _____ Areas that were not sustained are: _____ _____ _____ I think the reason(s) that this (these) learning(s)/ insight(s) was (were) not sustained is (are) likely that: _____ _____ _____	
Further comments: _____ _____ _____ *Please return by email* _____ *or fax* _____. *Thank you very much!*	

Assessment Tools

Another type of measurement, mentioned briefly in Chapter 3, is the use of an assessment tool, which is a common method (especially in organizations) for evaluating a range of behaviors, styles and other characteristics. Assessments may be introduced at the beginning of the coaching process to obtain a benchmark, or when it becomes evident to the coach that a client's conflict style and responses warrant further exploration that a known instrument provides.

Repeating the evaluation after the client has received coaching on the areas requiring improvement helps to assess changes and progress. Even a one-time use, though, provides material and relevant language for the coaching conversation about responses and conflict styles and yields important information relevant to developmental opportunities.

Assessment tools may be completed either by clients only, or "360-degree" instruments may be used. The latter require a number of people (more is better) to assess the client. These may include co-workers, bosses, direct reports and others who interact with and observe the client in conflictual situations. Multi-rater tools, which are useful for many reasons, provide particular assistance to clients who do not have a sense of how they are perceived and experienced by others. In either case, whether a client self-assessment or a 360-degree instrument is used, such tools are most effective if they include feedback to the client on the results, together with ongoing coaching that focuses on the areas for development.

Some other relevant things to consider about using assessment tools:

- Certification is required to be able to administer some tools.
- Instruments need to be psychometrically sound, valid and reliable.
- It is necessary that the person doing the assessment is skilled and provides concrete, supportive and helpful feedback.
- Instruments entail some cost, a notable point when budgeting for coaching.

- Tools can be overused. Many organizations use one or more to assess staff for career development, conflict behaviors/styles and interpersonal communication skills. Rather than overwhelm clients and staff with repeated 360-degree assessments, it is prudent to check whether any prior evaluations include indicators that may be applicable to conflict management coaching. The caveat is that coaches be certified in the use of such tools (when certification is required) before proceeding to provide feedback on the results as they apply to conflict management coaching to be done.
- The language and other variables regarding the assessment tool may not translate across cultures, countries and so on.
- When recommending the use of an assessment tool, it is important to ensure that clients are clear on what the instrument measures and how that pertains to the developmental areas they are to work on. This means describing how the results will help them gain awareness that was not realized or acknowledged before the assessment.
- For multi-rater instruments, staff members are generally reluctant to provide honest feedback, particularly in the narrative portions, unless they have an assurance of remaining anonymous. For this reason, using an online survey tool administered by an independent third party works well.
- Results of 360-degree instruments sometimes have skewed outcomes. Possibilities to keep in mind include whether the raters know the client well and whether they have observed the person in conflict, directly or otherwise. If they have little knowledge of the client, raters' answers may be based more on conjecture than experience or direct observation. Interpersonal or professional circumstances occurring at the time may also distort the results.
- Coaches and organizations may prefer to develop their own 360-degree surveys together with the client, sponsor and other stakeholders. These may be designed to consider the

specific areas of conflict management development relating to the client and the expectations of the workplace. Designing such instruments takes considerable skill to ensure soundness, reliability and validity.

- It is important before beginning an assessment process that the coach, client and sponsor are transparent regarding who will see the results and how they will be used. Some uses may be inappropriate (for example, to justify a dismissal).

A number of tools have been specifically designed for assessing conflict management behaviors and styles. Several are described briefly below.

Conflict Dynamics Profile®

The Conflict Dynamics Profile® (CDP) provides a method for clients to increase their awareness about their responses to conflict and what provokes them. The CDP is available online or in print format in a multi-rater (CDP-360) and an individual version (CDP-I). It is necessary that the coach be certified to use either format. This tool is psychometrically sound and has been validated. On completion of these instruments, the respondents receive a self-assessment report on their "Hot Buttons" and their constructive and destructive responses to conflict. The CDP-360 also includes a comprehensive conflict profile that provides measurement on:

- How others perceive the respondent's constructive and destructive responses to conflict.
- How the respondent responds before, during and after conflict and how he or she is perceived to do so.
- Which responses to conflict have the potential for harming one's position in the organization.

Persons being assessed using either the 360-degree or the individual instrument receive a useful booklet on managing conflict that provides tips and information about Hot Buttons and the various responses to conflict that the tool assesses, which are described next.

Constructive and Destructive Responses to Conflict

To rate responses to conflict according to the Conflict Dynamics Profile®, respondents and others assessing them for the 360-degree version indicate the frequency of a particular response along a five-point rating continuum from "never" to "always." The tool distinguishes constructive and destructive responses to conflict and also divides these responses into active and passive types, with specific behaviors ascribed to each. These categories are listed in Figure 7.6.

FIGURE 7.6 RESPONDING TO CONFLICT

Types of Responses	Definition	Specific Actions
Active–Constructive	Through some effort on the individual's part, the conflict and tension have been reduced.	Perspective taking Creating solutions Expressing emotions Reaching out
Passive–Constructive	Although there has not been overt action by the individual, the conflict has been dampened or de-escalated.	Reflective thinking Delay responding Adapting
Active–Destructive	Due to some action on the individual's part, the conflict has escalated.	Winning at all costs Displaying anger Demeaning others Retaliating
Passive–Destructive	Due to lack of effort or action, the individual causes conflict either to continue or to be resolved unsatisfactorily.	Avoiding Yielding Hiding emotions Self-criticizing

Source: Sal Capobianco, Mark Davis and Linda Kraus, *Managing Conflict Dynamics: A Practical Approach* (St. Petersburg, FL: Eckerd College, 2003), 3. Reprinted with permission of Eckerd College, The Center for Conflict Dynamics, St. Petersburg, FL.

Coaching clients who do the CDP-360 or CDP-I typically involves helping them to identify, examine and concentrate on improving behaviors that rate low for the constructive responses and high for the destructive ones. Another related coaching objective focuses on clients cooling their Hot Buttons.

Hot Buttons

The Hot Buttons, which only the respondent assesses in both the CDP-360 and CDP-I versions, are defined as follows:

- Unreliable—when people miss deadlines or cannot be counted on
- Overly analytical—when people focus too much on minor issues or are perfectionists
- Unappreciative—when people fail to give credit to others or seldom praise good performance
- Aloof—when people isolate themselves, do not seek input or are hard to approach
- Micro-managing—when people constantly monitor and check up on the work of others
- Self-centered—when people believe they are always correct or care only about themselves
- Abrasive—when people are arrogant, sarcastic and demeaning
- Untrustworthy—when people exploit others, take undeserved credit or cannot be trusted
- Hostile—when people lose their temper, become angry or yell at others[3]

Clients who do the CDP-360 also concentrate on any disparate perceptions between the raters' and respondent's rating of the latter's constructive and destructive responses and on a range of related organizational factors. Further, when establishing their coaching objectives, clients consider the narrative feedback provided by raters that focuses on areas for development.

Thomas–Kilmann Conflict Mode Instrument

The Thomas–Kilmann Instrument[4] (TKI) for measuring conflict styles was derived from theoretical models that relate the development of conflict styles to two underlying dimensions. One dimension is *assertiveness*, the desire to satisfy one's own concerns. The other dimension is *cooperativeness*, the desire to satisfy the other person's concerns. The extent to which the individual responds to situations between these two dimensions may be defined according to five specific modes of dealing with conflict:

> *Competing* is assertive and uncooperative, a power-oriented mode. When competing, an individual pursues his or her own concerns at the other person's expense, using whatever power seems appropriate to win his or her position. Competing might mean standing up for your rights, defending a position you believe is correct, or simply trying to win.
>
> *Collaborating* is both assertive and cooperative. When collaborating, an individual attempts to work with the other person to find a solution that fully satisfies the concerns of both. It involves digging into an issue to identify the underlying concerns of the two individuals and to find an alternative that meets both sets of concerns. Collaborating between two persons might take the form of exploring a disagreement to learn from each other's insights, resolving some condition that would otherwise have them competing for resources, or confronting and trying to find a creative solution to an interpersonal problem.
>
> *Compromising* is intermediate in both assertiveness and cooperativeness. When compromising, the objective is to find an expedient, mutually acceptable solution that partially satisfies both parties. Compromising falls on a middle ground between competing and accommodating, giving up more than competing but less than accommodating. Likewise, it addresses an issue more directly than avoiding but doesn't explore it in as

much depth as collaborating. Compromising might mean splitting the difference, exchanging concessions, or seeking a quick middle-ground position.

Avoiding is unassertive and uncooperative. When avoiding, an individual does not immediately pursue his or her own concerns or those of the other person. He or she does not address the conflict. Avoiding might take the form of diplomatically sidestepping an issue, postponing an issue until a better time, or simply withdrawing from a threatening situation.

Accommodating is unassertive and cooperative—the opposite of competing. When accommodating, an individual neglects his or her own concerns to satisfy the concerns of the other person; there is an element of self-sacrifice in this mode. Accommodating might take the form of selfless generosity or charity, obeying another person's order when you would prefer not to, or yielding to another's point of view.[5]

For this self-scoring tool, respondents answer a series of questions that help them gain awareness about their relative propensity to use some styles too much and others too little. Each conflict mode works best for some situations rather than others, depending on variables such as level of trust, importance of the issue to the person, quality of communication and listening skills, cultural influences including whether the culture supports an open dialogue and so on.

As a result of clients' discovery of which modes they are likely using too much, they recognize that other modes might be better for satisfying their own and others' needs. This often means considering which alternative conflict modes they have used too little. A balanced profile, with all scores in the moderate range, suggests that the respondent likely has a wider range of choices when in conflict and is able to apply the mode that best suits the situation.

An informative booklet accompanies the TKI questionnaire with explanations of a number of factors about each style, such as when each may and may not be useful. No certification or special qualification is required to administer this assessment.

Dealing with Conflict Instrument

Like the TKI, this tool gives respondents a better understanding of their conflict handling styles and presents the same five conflict styles—accommodate, avoid, compromise, compete and collaborate. By completing the Dealing with Conflict Instrument[6] (DWCI), respondents learn about their dominant style tendencies and the risks and opportunities of each, which are described in an accompanying booklet.

Respondents also analyze a specific dispute to determine which style is best for a given situation. They identify the conflict strategy that matches the scenario they have in mind along a spectrum that contemplates the importance of the outcome versus the importance of the relationship. In addition to the individual application, there is a DWCI 360-degree tool, which broadens the assessment by obtaining feedback from peers, managers, subordinates and others. Certification and special qualifications for administration are not required.

Coaching using this assessment generally addresses the same objectives as described regarding the TKI.

Suggestions for Research

There are many areas for future research regarding conflict management coaching. Developing qualitative and quantitative criteria and methods for measuring effectiveness of this process, whichever model is used, are two of these.

Other possible research areas:

- A comparison of outcomes, user satisfaction and other variables based on using a third-party intervention and a one-on-one process for helping people manage their conflicts and disputes.
- A comparison of the sustainability of learning and skills gained in conflict management training, measured with and

without the addition of individualized coaching before and after the workshop.

- The impact of pre-mediation conflict management coaching by separate coaches for each party, considering variables such as outcome of the mediation, level of participation, durability of conflict management skills gained, process satisfaction, outcome satisfaction, the parties' confidence and other factors.*

- How the attendance of coaches during mediation may affect factors such as the level and effectiveness of disputing parties' participation, the outcome of mediation, process satisfaction, what parties learn and sustain regarding conflict management, their confidence and other variables.*

- The types of intervention that are best suited considering the neurobiology of conflict escalation and de-escalation, as well as neuroscience principles that have an impact on coaching individuals through their interpersonal conflicts and disputes.

- Proficiencies for conflict management coaching that may inform standards of practice for pertinent training.

- Cultural factors to consider when providing conflict management coaching.

- Ways to inspire the use of conflict management coaching in organizations as a proactive mechanism to help people engage more effectively in conflict.

- How conflict management coaching is applied in private and public sector organizations and what the critical success factors are.

---

* The type of mediation is also a factor to be considered.

SUMMARY

- The type of measurement used to assess the effectiveness of conflict management coaching depends on factors such as the purpose, who and what are being evaluated and how the results will be used.

- Measuring the success of conflict management coaching on an organizational basis includes assessing the return on investment. This requires a quantitative evaluation of variables such as whether coaching precludes more costly interventions and the effect on retention, absenteeism and productivity.

- Because clients experience progress subjectively, qualitative measurement is also important in evaluating the success of coaching. Qualitative outcomes include such factors as whether clients reach their objectives, the impact of coaching on the client and on the work unit, how clients sustain their learning and apply their insights to future conflicts and other variables.

- Questionnaires with rating scales, face-to-face discussion and a combination of these and other methods are useful in gaining and compiling data to assess the effectiveness of conflict management coaching. Similarly, assessing the process and the coach during and after coaching is completed helps to evaluate coaching.

- Assessment tools may be used in conflict management coaching as one way to focus the process, to measure progress or both. Several instruments concentrate specifically on conflict behavior and styles. Such tools indicate areas requiring development and provide useful language for coaches and clients to employ. Assessments of this nature may be used once or repeatedly during the coaching process, or after it ends, as a way to benchmark and evaluate progress.

- Conflict management coaching is a relatively new specialty in the coaching, ADR, HR and leadership fields. Research on a range of areas will help to measure its effectiveness, add to its legitimacy and develop more applications.

Notes

1. See Tammy Lenski, "The Case for Conflict Coaching" (January 6, 2010), http://conflictzen.lenski.com/conflict-coaching-return-on-investment.

2. http://www.conflictdynamics.org.

3. Craig Runde and Tim Flanagan, *Becoming a Conflict Competent Leader: How You and Your Organization Can Manage Conflict Effectively* (San Francisco: Jossey-Bass, 2007), 42. Reprinted with permission of John Wiley & Sons, Inc.

4. http://www.kilmann.com/conflict.html.

5. Kenneth W. Thomas and Ralph H. Kilmann, *Thomas–Kilmann Conflict Mode Instrument* (Mountain View, CA: CPP, 2007), 8. Modified and reproduced by special permission of the Publisher, CPP, Inc., Mountain View, CA 94043 from Thomas-Kilmann Conflict Mode Instrument by Kenneth W. Thomas and Ralph H. Kilmann. Copyright 1974, 2002, 2007 and 2011 by CPP, Inc. All rights reserved. Further reproduction is prohibited without the Publisher's written consent.

6. http://www.hrdpress.com/Catalog/Conflict-Mgmt-Assessments. In addition, other conflict-related assessment tools include the Kraybill Conflict Style Inventory (http://riverhouseepress.com) and the Intercultural Conflict Style Inventory (http://www.icsinventory.com).

Appendixes

APPENDIX I   Ways That Coaching Compares to Consulting, Counseling/Therapy and Mentoring

Coaching*	Consulting	
Focus		
The coaching focus is on helping people gain awareness and new perspectives to make changes that optimize their potential in their personal or professional lives. Among other things, coaching is premised on self-determination and client-generated solutions, choices and possibilities.	Consultants are experts on certain subject matters. Their focus is on making assessments and providing suggestions and advice for organizational/business solutions, according to their areas of expertise. Personal consultants similarly operate with this focus. Some coaching specialties combine coaching and consulting based on the expertise of the coach/consultant.	
Method		
The method is conversational and informal. Sessions may be conducted face to face, by Internet, telephone or video. Generally speaking, coaches use a collaborative method to co-create the coach–client relationship. They employ questioning and other skills that help clients increase their self-awareness and insights needed to reach their objectives. Coaches also provide support, structure and feedback to help clients shift thinking, attitudes and conduct. Coaching requires clients to identify and take concrete actions to achieve their goals. Coaches challenge clients to stretch themselves to do more than they might do on their own.	There is typically a level of formality in the relationship. Communication may be conducted face to face; however, other formats may be used. Consultants listen to the issues of concern, ask questions, explore the organization's or person's needs, assess the overall and specific situation and provide advice and opinions to the people and organizations who retain them to provide their expertise.	

Counseling/Therapy**	Mentoring
Counseling and therapy are commonly focused on healing emotional wounds and on helping people resolve the historical sources of their current state of mind and heart. This typically involves identifying and discussing the issues and emotions that interfere with the individual's ability to function effectively. Counselors and therapists also help people gain increased understanding and awareness of themselves and their situation. Licensed practitioners determine/diagnose and treat pathology; psychiatrists dispense medication, if needed.	In workplaces, mentors are experienced people, such as senior staff members or retirees of the organization. They generally focus on helping leaders and others, referred to as "partners," to gain specific skills, to advance their professional path and to otherwise learn information, strategies and tools relevant to their career development. Mentoring is essentially a learning activity.
There is typically a level of formality in the relationship. Sessions may be conducted face to face; however, other formats may be used. In addition to listening and encouraging clients to talk out their issues, therapists and counselors help clients to generate insights and solutions to their problems. Counselors and therapists provide support and may share their views, insights and ideas.	There are varying levels of formality that depend on the mentor's style, the organizational culture and other factors. Communication is mostly face to face; however, other formats may be used. In organizations/workplaces, mentors listen to staff members' goals and provide them with information, advice, counsel and guidance based on their own experiences and knowledge. Mentors also identify and share what they observe as areas for the partner's development, e.g., leadership, succession planning.

Coaching*	Consulting	
Time orientation		
Present situation and future plans.	Present situation and future plans.	
Assumptions by practitioner about the persons seeking assistance		
Clients are creative and resourceful. With the coach's support, questions and observations, they gain increased awareness and different perspectives. With coaching, clients are also able to tap into their natural strengths and potential in their efforts to reach their goals.	Clients expect the consultant to provide professional expert advice.	
Length of sessions		
Variable and co-created by the client and coach.	As needed by client and/or organization.	
Frequency/Duration		
Weekly, bi-monthly or other frequency, as mutually agreed by client and coach, and for a duration that meets the objectives and/or the organization's or client's budgeting constraints.	As required to complete the consultation and/or implementation, subject to budget constraints.	
Agenda		
The agenda essentially belongs to clients and is aimed at achieving their objectives. When workplaces refer clients, the agenda may also be in accordance with the organization's objectives. Coaches typically follow a coaching model/framework that facilitates clients' progress and goal attainment.	The agenda is set by the client/organization and often develops with the consultant's observations and input.	

Counseling/Therapy**	Mentoring
Past, present and future-oriented (in varying degrees, depending on type of practice).	Present situation and future plans.
Clients are seeking help to heal psychologically and to move beyond blocks. Some clients' behaviors are found to be dysfunctional.	Partners are willing and able to learn from the mentor.
Typically, scheduled for specific time periods on a regular basis.	Variable and planned by the mentor and partner.
Short- and long-term durations; may depend on cost, insurance coverage and other variables, including the type of intervention provided. In some cases, psychiatric interventions last for years.	According to need and parameters of the mentoring program or the plan developed by the mentor and partner.
The agenda is often directed by the counselor/therapist, depending on the type of counseling/therapy.	The agenda is directed by the partner, who identifies the goals and what he or she wants to learn or gain with the mentor's assistance.

Coaching*	Consulting	
Clients		
Clients may be leaders or others who are ready, willing and able to focus on, and gain increased awareness and competence about, ways of improving aspects of their lives. People are also referred to coaching. Under those circumstances, some clients may be less ready, willing and able than others to participate, at least initially.	Organizations are the clients who require expert advice on specific and identifiable matters. Individuals may also be clients who request consulting services in the form of advice and opinions for particular areas of their lives about which the consultant is an expert.	
Compensation		
There is no fee for internal coaches. For external practitioners there is a fee for coaching, which varies depending on the coach's experience, credentials, background and education. Fees may be based on an hourly rate or block period, e.g., monthly.	The amount and method consultants charge for their services may be based on an hourly rate or other payment arrangement. Expertise, experience, education and background often have an impact on the amount of the fees.	

Counseling/Therapy**	Mentoring
Known as "patients" by psychiatrists and some psychologists and psycho-therapists, those who seek or are referred to counseling/therapy may be in emotional distress and/or immobi-lized in various ways that impede healthy relationships, decision-making, problem-solving, progress and so on. There may be a psychological pathol-ogy for which they are being treated.	Mostly, organizations identify staff members who are likely to benefit from mentoring to gain specific skills and knowledge and optimize their potential.
Health insurance pays for medical practitioners (psychiatrists). Some benefit plans, insurance policies and Employee Assistance Programs defray all or part of a specified number of hours for psychologists, counselors and therapists. Fees for practitioners who do not fall under certain categories or are not covered by benefit plans generally charge on an hourly basis.	There are no fees for mentoring.

    *   For the purposes of the comparisons in this table, the category of coaching pertains to coaching in general, not specifically conflict management coaching.

  ** The categories of counseling and therapy are combined, and the word therapy is used for the purposes of the comparisons listed. These are general descrip-tions and acknowledge that there are various types of counseling, therapy and psychotherapy.

APPENDIX II Some General Differences Between Conflict Management Coaching and Mediation

The following table describes general comparisons, recognizing that there are different types of mediation and conflict management coaching, and different practitioners' styles for conducting these processes.

Conflict Management Coaching	Mediation
Objectives	
• A conflict management coach works with one person who aims to manage a past or ongoing dispute independently. The client may also wish to prepare for a potentially contentious matter or process, including a mediation. Further, coaches help clients who want to increase their conflict competence in general, so that they are able to respond to and engage more effectively in conflict.	• A mediator works together with two or more parties who aim to discuss and resolve their specific differences, which may be about issues in dispute between or among them. Depending on the type of mediation and the mediator's style, the focus may also (or instead) be on relationship matters.
Practitioner's role	
• An informal conversational forum is used in which the coach's questions and other skills aim to advance clients' self-discovery to inspire different perspectives and to motivate their actions for reaching their conflict management objectives.	• A conversational forum is used in which the mediator's questions and other skills aim to advance resolution of the parties' dispute and/or reconciliation of their relationship. Mediation tends to be more formal than one-on-one coaching.

Conflict Management Coaching	Mediation
Process	
• The stages of coaching are generally geared to increasing clients' self-awareness and gaining knowledge, skills and abilities to attain their conflict management goals.	• The stages of mediation are generally geared to facilitating problem-solving discussions and/or mending the parties' relationship, including ways of communicating.
Empowerment	
• The coaching process is meant to be empowering for clients and assist them to optimize their potential regarding their specific objectives.	• Mediation may be empowering for the parties. Some forms of mediation are intentionally designed to be so.
Duration	
• Conflict management coaching commonly involves a series of weekly sessions for up to 60 minutes each. The duration depends on variables such as the client's goals and budget constraints.	• Mediation commonly involves one or a limited number of meetings for two or more hours per session. Some mediation sessions may last a day at a time. The duration varies depending on the context and other factors.
Voluntariness	
• Coaching is meant to be a voluntary process, though some clients referred to coaching may be reluctant to participate and perceive they have no choice (this topic is discussed in detail in Chapter 3).	• Mediation is meant to be a voluntary process (though there are mandatory court-connected mediation programs). Some parties may be reluctant to participate and perceive they have no choice.

Conflict Management Coaching	Mediation
Tasks	
• In conflict management coaching, clients commonly do a task or tasks pertinent to their objectives between sessions.	• There may be tasks for the disputing parties to do that are related to the issues being mediated, if there is more than one mediation session.
Agreement to participate	
• Coaches may use either a written or verbal contract containing terms such as roles, responsibilities, confidentiality, voluntariness and so on (see, e.g., Chapter 3, Figure 3.3, "Conflict Management Coaching Agreement").	• There is usually a written Agreement to Mediate that contains terms regarding confidentiality and voluntariness and other provisions regarding the mediation process.
Written summary	
• There is no written summary of the outcomes of coaching.	• The mediator typically provides a written summary of the outcomes of mediation, e.g., Minutes of Settlement.

Note: Within the discussion on Applications, Chapter 6 outlines some similarities between conflict management coaching and mediation. Figure 6.1 in that chapter also provides an overview of general comparisons between pre-mediation sessions as a coach for a party and the mediator with points that are relevant to the content of this Appendix.

APPENDIX III   Some Common Words Describing Emotional Responses Triggered by Another Person's Actions or Words

Abandoned	Depressed	Hurt	Puzzled
Admonished	Despairing	Impatient	Regretful
Affronted	Despondent	Incensed	Rejected
Afraid	Devastated	Incited	Resentful
Agitated	Diminished	Incredulous	Resistant
Ambushed	Disappointed	Insecure	Sad
Angry	Disbelieving	Insulted	Scared
Annoyed	Disconcerted	Intimidated	Self-doubting
Anxious	Discouraged	Irritated	Shamed
Ashamed	Disgruntled	Jilted	Shocked
Attacked	Disgusted	Lost	Sick
Betrayed	Distressed	Mad	Sorrowful
Bitter	Disturbed	Manipulated	Startled
Blamed	Embarrassed	Miserable	Stressed
Blindsided	Enraged	Misunderstood	Stunned
Bullied	Fearful/	Mournful	Surprised
Challenged	Frightened	Nervous	Suspicious
Chastised	Frustrated	Neglected	Tearful
Concerned	Furious	Offended	Threatened
Confronted	Grief-stricken	Outraged	Undermined
Confused	Guilty	Overwhelmed	Uneasy
Contemptuous	Hateful	Pained	Unnerved
Cornered	Heartbroken	Panicked	Unsettled
Crushed	Helpless	Perturbed	Upset
Defensive	Hopeless	Pressured	Vulnerable
Deflated	Horrified	Provoked	Wary
Degraded	Hostile	Punished	Worried
Dejected	Humiliated	Put down	Wronged

APPENDIX IV   Common Fears Expressed in Workplace Conflicts/Disputes

Alienation

Becoming aggressive

Becoming violent

Being bullied

Being perceived as a complainer

Being seen/perceived in ways I don't want to be

Being wrong

Change

Continuing to be faced with unmet needs, no answers, lack of satisfaction

Depth of emotion—own and the other's

Emotional pain

Failure

Hurt

Isolation

Loss of employment benefits

Loss of certainty

Loss of choice/autonomy

Loss of confidence

Loss of connection

Loss of control

Loss of decision-making

Loss of emotional control

Loss of face

Loss of job or demotion

Loss of love, affection

Loss of money/income

Loss of physical control

Loss of position, status (identity)

Loss of power

Loss of privilege

Loss of relationships/friends

Loss of respect

Loss of self-esteem

Loss of stability/security

Loss of status

Loss of support

Nothing changing for the better

Physical pain

Possible violence on the other person's part

Rage and hostility—own and the other's

Rejection

Retaliation

The other person's aggressiveness

The unknown

Unpredictable behavior on the other person's part

Unpredictable/irrational behavior on my part

Index

Cinnie Noble, CM, BSW, LLM(ADR), ACC, CMed, is a pioneer in the development of conflict management coaching. As a lawyer and certified coach and mediator with extensive experience in the fields of conflict management and executive coaching, Cinnie brought together principles from these two major disciplines to create the CINERGY™ model in 1999. Since that time, she is regularly asked to speak internationally on this subject and also writes extensively about the model's numerous applications. Cinnie and her associates coach people in many parts of the world and also train others worldwide to use this unique coaching method.

Cinnie has taught conflict management courses at the University of Windsor Law School, University of Toronto and York University, and is a guest lecturer in the Masters of Law program in Alternate Dispute Resolution at Osgoode Hall Law School. Two of the four books she has written to date are on the subject of mediation: *Mediation Advocacy: Effective Client Representation in Mediation Proceedings* (with co-authors Leslie Dizgun and Paul Emond; Emond Montgomery, 1998) and *Family Mediation: A Guide for Lawyers* (Canada Law Book, 1999). She also recently co-authored with Ed Modell and Diane Brennan the chapter "Conflict Management" in *The Handbook of Knowledge-Based Coaching* by Leni Wildflower and Diane Brennan (Jossey-Bass, 2011).

Cinnie is a former board member of the Greater Toronto Area chapter of the International Coach Federation. She co-founded and is the current host of ICF's Conflict Management Coaching—Special Interest Group. Cinnie also founded and currently chairs the Conflict Coaching Committee of the Association for Conflict Resolution's Workplace Section.

Cinnie was appointed a Member of the Order of Canada in 1991.

For More Information on CINERGY™ Coaching

CINERGY™ Coaching is a division of Noble Solutions Inc., based in Toronto, Canada. We provide one-on-one conflict management coaching worldwide and also train others to use our model in different parts of the world. Our training programs, some of which are conducted by telecourse, include:

- Conflict Management Coaching Workshop
- Conflict Management Coaching Advanced Workshop
- Leader as Conflict Management Coach
- Share Model of Collaborative Family Law Coaching
- Designing and Promoting Conflict Management Coaching Programs for Organizations
- ConflictMastery™

More information about our workshops may be found at our website: http://www.cinergycoaching.com.

We also have a conflict management coaching blog at http://www.cinergycoaching.com/blog/.

CINERGY™ has a program for accrediting trainers, and only those designated as CINERGY™ Accredited Trainers may conduct workshops that train people to use this model. We welcome inquiries from people who wish to obtain the requisite skills and join our team. CINERGY™ also has partners around the world who license our workshops, and we welcome your interest in this regard.

Please feel free to visit our website or contact us for more information on our coaching and training services at **info@cinergycoaching.com**.

CPSIA information can be obtained
at www.ICGtesting.com
Printed in the USA
LVHW051514111121
703079LV00012B/1124

9 780987 739407